# THEOLOGY AND PREACHING

# THEOLOGY
## AND
# PREACHING

A programme of work in
dogmatics, arranged with
reference to Questions 1-11
of the Heidelberg Catechism

*by*

HEINRICH OTT

*Translated by*
*Harold Knight*

THE WESTMINSTER PRESS
PHILADELPHIA

Library of Congress Catalog Card No. 65-12513

*Published by The Westminster Press*
*Philadelphia, Pennsylvania* ®
*Printed in Great Britain*

# CONTENTS

5

CONTENTS

# Part Two

## CLARIFICATION OF THE PROGRAMME IN THE LIGHT OF THE DOCTRINE OF SIN

## POSTSCRIPT

*The Revised Standard Version of the Bible has been followed in quotations*

# TRANSLATOR'S NOTE
## ON THE TITLE

THE EXACT translation of the German title is "Dogmatics and Proclamation", neither of which terms, as currently used in continental theology, is at once familiar to the Anglo-Saxon reader. "Dogmatics" has a much narrower meaning than "theology": it implies the crystallization in sharply defined formulae of the substance of the Christian revelation, and with special reference to the experience of that revelation in the general Christian consciousness. "Proclamation" means simply the declaration of the original Christian message of salvation, and implies especially the impact of that message on some living concrete situation of the moment; it is an activity in which the immediacy and relevance of the unchanging kerygma is illuminated afresh. The author of this work studies the interaction and interconnexion of the two activities.

# INTRODUCTION

THIS BOOK contains in revised form a series of lectures which I gave both at the University of Basel in the winter of 1958/59 and also at the University of Bonn in the winter of 1960/61, where I took the place of the late Professor Hans Joachim Iwand.

Like my *Eschatologie* (1958) this study is intended to lay before the reader a programme of dogmatic work: it puts forward a deeply considered proposition as to how future dogmatic reflection can and should proceed, while at the same time, by way of example, it supplies a partial fulfilment of this dogmatic programme.

Both in regard to the present work, and to my *Eschatologie*, I am fully conscious of the need for an amplification and improvement of what I have done. But in theology we must make the venture—and today perhaps more than ever—of saying something tentatively and provisionally in fufilment of our designs. We must bear well in mind the truth that theology is and remains a *theologia viatorum*, of pilgrims. If we did not take it upon ourselves to speak in the consciousness that what we say is provisional only, then theological discussion—and theology *is* after all a discussion—would never start. What is important, however, is that we should not speak at random and that we should not cling obstinately to given dogmatic positions either of the present or the past, but that we should try to make certain, with constantly renewed efforts to be serious and methodical, that our theological endeavour grows out of the one abiding mission of the Church of Jesus Christ, and takes fully into account also the special problems of the time in which we live.

Theology must progress. In this aeon there is no such thing as a final theology. In the future, no doubt, we shall become partakers of the *theologia gloriae*, of the knowledge which is proper to God Himself, and in His light we shall "know, as we are known" (1 Cor. 13:12). But until this time comes, dogmatic thought must start afresh in each generation and yet in its ever-renewed initiatives it must remain faithful to the *communio sanctorum*, the communion of saints of all ages, to the great theological tradition which can never be superseded but must remain for us ever alive and fresh. I shall never forget Karl Barth, on the occasion of the great celebration oi his 70th birthday in Basel, warning us younger men that in dogmatics we must not work to attain a Barthian scholasticism, in which we might be content within the given broad framework of his writings to argue about petty particular points, but that we should now strive to carry the process of dogmatic thinking a stage further.

The general direction in which such further progress should now take place has been suggested by Barth himself in repeated indications and programmatic remarks, and with special forcefulness in his lecture on the humanity of God (*Theol. Studien*, 48, 1956). This direction is suggested in the phrase: *a turning towards man himself.* Barth thinks that in this connexion it is a question of a "genuine retractation", which

> consists by no means in a subsequent return to former positions, but in a new initiative and attack, in which what has been said before is to be said again all the more forcibly, only better more appropriately. If what we then expressed and thought we had discovered (*sc.* "that God is God") was no final message, but a message in need of retractation, yet it was a true message which as such must abide, which today cannot be eluded, but which must rather form the presupposition of what has now to be thought out (*op. cit.* p. 7).

If in the following study I endeavour to develop the programme of dogmatic work out of the essential co-ordination of the latter with church proclamation, I consider that in so doing I am remaining faithful to the spirit of Barth's own work, for his "dialectical theology", according to his own early and probably still valid understanding of himself, grew out of the situation by which the preacher is faced. And at the same time, I believe that I am taking a small step forward in the direction in which Barth suggested that dogmatics should proceed; for, where preaching is the guiding point of view, it is pre-eminently a question of the event of *human understanding*, and furthermore, of human understanding of the word of *God*. Thus, under the guidance of the preacher's point of view, the "turning towards man himself" might well be exemplified, and the "humanity of God" effectively brought out.

This could happen without the slightest suggestion of a "subsequent return to former positions". For it is just the *verbum alienum* of the living God, the word of Another, that is proclaimed in the word of the preacher. *God Himself* speaks. But after saying this, the "first word", we must point out that today the important thing is to consider the repercussions of the divine word in the sphere of human realities—and where otherwise is the word of God to be found by us? The important thing is, to use an expression sometimes used by Barth himself, to work towards achieving a "Theology of the Holy Spirit", which tries to say once more the same thing (and nothing else!) but which tries to say it from the point of view of man.

This turning to a new point of view is today essential. For, after theology rediscovered its enduring basis in the great crisis of the twenties, it now sees itself faced by an abundance of problems which lie on the horizontal, the human plane. And it should be noted that these problems are no marginal problems for church and theology; they form fields of debate in which theology, with its own most special mission, must prove its worth. How urgent such questions are may be plainly seen in ecumenical discussions and in the present position of the young churches in Asia and Africa, which have to understand the same gospel of Jesus Christ in a human-historical environment so basically different from that of western Christianity, and in those very different conditions to live it out and to bring its message to bear effectively on the concrete features of daily life. What is now to be done in grappling with the problems just mentioned may not be done casually, marginally, as "theological literature", but must be done in the spirit of serious theology. We shall hardly make progress with these great tasks which await us and which have not yet been mastered if we do not succeed, from the start, in thrusting through to man himself, in a serious (that is, strictly methodical) manner, and not in the style of the aphoristic essay, "painting pictures on water" as Anselm of Canterbury put it; and then, from the understanding of man and in full view of the phenomena of human reality, unfold and amplify the word of *God*.

In all this, it is a question first—and perhaps in the main —of what is involved in human understanding. What are the possibilities of man and where lie the limits of his understanding? What can be understood and what not? We must not grow weary of emphasizing, and in the most different directions too, that man cannot know this in advance! Whoever thinks he can settle in advance what is understandable has not yet apprehended the problem of understanding. Hermeneutics (in the broadest sense) cannot be restricted by any anthropological doctrine. A complete system of hermeneutics as the basis for all understanding can in no wise be framed. The problem of hermeneutics is and must remain posed (even though some circles of Barthians avoid facing this and would only too willingly prefer to be finally satisfied with what has been attained). In this respect Dietrich Bonhoeffer is right in declaring:

> A word can only be authoritatively and convincingly spoken to me when it springs from the deepest knowledge of my humanity and strikes me here and now in the total reality of my human existence. Any other kind of word is powerless. Hence the Church's message to the world, if it is to be authoritative and convincing, must be declared with the deepest knowledge of the world's life and must concern the world in the full scope of its present reality.

Again, he is right when he asks:

> How can the Gospel, how can the offer of the Church be proclaimed with power, that is to say, with the utmost actuality and persuasiveness? (*Ges. Schr.* I, pp. 144ff.)

And again, when he finally sees himself to be

> utterly forced back upon the very beginnings of understanding: What is called atonement and redemption, regeneration and the Holy Spirit, love of one's enemy, the cross and the

resurrection, life in Christ and the following of Christ, all that is so hard to understand and so remote that we hardly dare to speak of it any more. In the words and the actions which have been handed down to us by tradition, we surmise something utterly new and revolutionary, without however being able as yet to understand and express it (*Widerstand und Ergebung*, p. 26).

If we basically agree with Bonhoeffer in all this, and regard his experience, his questioning and his vision as decisively orientating the position of the theological problem and the shape of the theological task in our time, then we shall leave aside as irrelevant and inappropriate the idea of a world which has grown up, an idea which has today gained currency as a theory in philosophical history.

In this connexion a meeting with Rudolf Bultmann as man and teacher has been of the greatest importance to me. It is he who with extreme force and urgency has brought us inescapably face to face with the hermeneutical problem. Whatever be our attitude in detail to the hermeneutical teachings of Bultmann (which he himself can hardly regard as conclusive and final) we shall not be able to argue away the existence of the problem itself. Different moreover as are the theologians Barth and Bultmann in the style of their thought, the framing of their questions, their backgrounds, their conclusions and their outlooks (and also in the behaviour of their pupils), at one point—and it could well be the decisive one—they are none the less united: for both of them the main question is of God's word, which is a living word and no abstract idea. Both, therefore, are concerned about the genuine summons of the real God to real human beings.

To Bultmann I owe the impulsion to inquire into the matter of theological ontology, or rather, ontological questions in theology; I owe to him the insight that this question must be faced if, under the broadly understood heading of hermeneutics, we wish to turn to consider the reality of man confronted by the reality of the living God. Rightly understood, hermeneutics and ontology are bound up with each other in the closest possible way. Hermeneutically we inquire into the specific *modus loquendi*, the mode of speaking (and therewith into the "whence") of the individual Biblical testimonies; ontologically we inquire into the specific *modus essendi*, the mode of being, of the reality to which they testify. We shall not succeed in achieving the break-through to the real man, unanimously postulated by Barth, Bonhoeffer and Bultmann, if we neglect these two closely interconnected questions. Instead, in this respect, we should have to remain at the stage of theological literature, at the stage of pictures painted on water!

There can be no question, in pursuing either the hermeneutic or the ontological enquiry, of using any preconceived philosophical premises. This, unfortunately, is all too often misunderstood, and as a consequence discussions are made unnecessarily difficult. What we have to maintain rather is just the freedom of theological thought from any sort of philosophical substructure—a freedom which is not merely asserted but which is really exercised in critical reflection. If we keep firmly before us the hermeneutical and ontological points of view, suspending all hard and fast philosophical premises, the "thing itself" in theology will make its voice heard. This does not exclude but includes constant *contact* with philosophy.

In the framework of this wide-reaching theological programme, the following essay can of course represent only a small advance. It follows the text of the Heidelberg Catechism and thus links itself with a great theological tradition. It puts forward nothing "new" but proposes essentially to justify the catechism and its teaching about sin. Its purpose will have been fulfilled, if it succeeds in showing that proclamation as a guiding point of view in dogmatic work is meaningful and helpful as well as being productive of greater clarity and concrete actuality and relevance; and if, further, it shows that the hermeneutical and ontological points of departure lead not to empty abstractions and formalisms but to the richness and breadth of theological tradition with its great problems, and to the richness and breadth of human reality, in regard to which it is our duty to fulfil the commission laid upon us by our Lord.

*Arisdorf, December 1960*　　　　　　　　HEINRICH OTT

# PART ONE
## THE PROGRAMME

# CHAPTER I

# DOGMATICS AS A GUIDE TO PREACHING

## 1. *Dogmatics, Preaching and the Church*

THE THEME of our inquiry springs out of the definition of dogmatics itself. It is well known that Karl Barth described theology, and dogmatics in particular, in such wise as to attribute to it an office of supervision, the supervision in fact of gospel proclamation. It is the duty of theology to see that the Church's current proclamation of the Word remains faithful to its concrete task and the documentation of that task in Holy Scripture. It assesses current proclamation or preaching by the criterion of its object, as this object is testified in the word of scripture. Thus in a certain sense it stands midway between the Bible and actual church preaching.

This viewpoint applies pre-eminently to dogmatics. For while Biblical theology stresses and clarifies the statements of the Biblical documents themselves, and to that extent stands "nearer" to the Bible, whereas practical theology on the other hand tests the Church's fulfilment of its preaching mission and moves closer to that mission, dogmatics properly occupies a position between the two, a conspicuously mediatorial position, which becomes the decisive characteristic of all theological undertaking. Dogmatics is the highest stage of the reflection which constitutes the essence of theology. It is of course essential to reflective thought that it proceeds by stages. For there is indeed a process of reflecting on reflection, meditating on meditation, and that necessarily so.[1] Dogmatics then forms the highest stage of theological reflection, for it meditates on the

---

[1] Of course this process by which reflection lifts itself above itself cannot be continued *ad infinitum*. Somewhere thought must come to rest. It would be most interesting to investigate more deeply some time this philosophical—and theological—question of the structure of thought!

conclusions of study and meditation, in so far for example as it ponders the appropriateness or otherwise of the processes of exegetical or practical theology. In dogmatics true Christian teaching springs into life as an event, and in this way above all the churchly supervisory office of theology is fulfilled.

Of course it must be said here that the lines of demarcation between dogmatics and exegetical and practical theology are fluid. These three essential disciplines of theology (church history is probably to be regarded as an indispensable auxiliary to all three and thus essentially presents itself as the history of exegesis, the history of dogma and the history of gospel proclamation) form at bottom one sole continuum of reflection which stretches from the Biblical testimonies to the Church's preaching mission. The culmination and the centre of this process however lies at the point where "dogmatic" questions in the narrow sense are posed. It is precisely this central position and the fact just mentioned of the continuity of the process which made it possible in the earliest times of evangelical theology to neglect, in a certain sense, the discipline of dogmatics and to exalt Biblical theology as the all-controlling and leading theological discipline. There have been times when, at the theological faculties, there were professorial chairs only in the Old and New Testaments. At such times Biblical theology included dogmatic sequences of thought and practical, pastoral considerations. Hence instruction in it could rightly be seen as a valid formation of both theologians and pastors. In fact and truth it must be said that basically dogmatics is to be found everywhere in theological thinking. Every theological question contains in the last resort the specifically dogmatic question concerning the "doctrine"; that is to say, the question of rightly understanding what is to be proclaimed.

Thus dogmatics is, according to the above definition by Karl Barth (and to this definition little objection can be made), a specific function of the Church. Dogmatics is no abstract teaching engaged in for its own sake. The "life-situation" of dogmatics is the Church. Dogmatics exists and must exist only because of the existence of the Church. In so far as the preaching of the gospel is a constitutive function of the Church (and there is no church without gospel proclamation; the Church is essentially the sphere where the gospel is proclaimed; to declare the gospel is the Church's business) gospel proclamation and theology are most closely interrelated. The co-ordination of theology and the Church is effected through gospel proclamation. Thus in connexion with Karl Barth I once sought to define theology (and hence more particularly dogmatics) as "the reflective function of preaching itself". I would like to make this definition the basis of all that is to follow.

The question of the relation between preaching and dogmatics should be the decisive question both in preaching and in dogmatics itself. Dogmatics has constantly to take into consideration the process of gospel proclamation, because only in relation to this process does it find its life. But the preacher must ever and again inquire what is to be proclaimed, hence what is the "object" of proclamation, hence what is the true "doctrine" which constitutes that object, hence in fact he must concern himself with dogmatics. In considering their mutual relationship, dogmatics and preaching first come to the knowledge of themselves, become aware of their own true place, function and being.

### 2. Continuity between Preaching and Dogmatics

On the assumption of these basic principles, we have further to inquire into the mode of this intimate relationship between preaching and dogmatics. When we say that dogmatics is the reflective aspect of preaching itself, then the act of the Church in preaching and theology appears necessarily as one single act, a single deed—except that on the one occasion it is "immediate" and on the other "reflective". Preaching and dogmatics are in the last resort a single activity of the Church, two aspects of one and the same thing.

I would like to qualify the truth which here dawns upon us as the continuity between preaching and dogmatics. In order that we may make clear to ourselves the full extent of this insight, let us consider the present theological situation. At all times all true theology has moved in this continuity, in such wise, for example, that in its characteristic language its nexus with preaching has been manifest (we have only to think for example of Calvin's *Institutes*, Augustine's *Confessions*, Luther's *Of the Freedom of a Christian Man*). Today we are confronted by the noteworthy fact that a theological tendency has arisen, which in itself truly deserves to be described as essentially theology, which, however, emphatically denies the fact of this continuity. I am referring to demythologization—that is, the self-understanding of theology which lies behind the theological programme of demythologizing.

How does the theology of demythologization understand itself as theological science? In this connexion Ernst Fuchs (*Hermeneutik*, 1954, pp. 98ff.) says very appropriately:

> A quarrel has arisen among us which concerns precisely the scientific character of theology considered as conceptual doctrine. This quarrel concerns primarily the process of demythologizing the New Testament proclamation. . . . As is known, it is feared that Bultmann's way of speaking theologically will result in an impoverishment of the contents and the fullness of revelation. But this implies a confusion between doctrine and preaching or the life of faith. The task of dogmatics is in the first instance a supervisory one. For there is a difference between my imparting to others the divine revelation and my meditating on the truth of this communication in the context of human language. . . . Theology is . . . not preaching, but presupposes preaching as a communication of revelation; it inquires into the *possibility* of such a communication as an activity of man. Hence theology ought not to propose to itself to declare the fullness of revelation!

These sentences from Fuchs' *Hermeneutik* are a *locus classicus* for that self-understanding of theology which is linked to the process of demythologization. They in fact express the opinion of Bultmann himself. No doubt Bultmann too—and certainly his pupil Fuchs—sees theology in close connexion with preaching. It is there for the sake of preaching. So much is plain, too, from the above quotation from Fuchs. But everything very much depends on how this close connexion is understood and defined. For two different things are involved, whether we speak only of a belonging together or whether we speak of a continuity between preaching and theology. In any event, Fuchs, in the wake of Bultmann, defines the connexion of the two in such a way as to exclude any continuity. It is at least clear from the above quotation that the controversy only superficially concerns the question of demythologization, that on a deeper level it is a controversy about the programme which theology should set itself. This situation will soon become evident to anyone who can grasp the interconnexion of the problems. It is also right to say that demythologization proceeds from an understanding of theology which sharply discriminates between theology and preaching. The objection to Bultmann, often heard, that he impoverishes the "fullness of revelation", stems of course, according to Fuchs, from a "misunderstanding", from a "confusion between doctrine and preaching or the life of faith". Theology in contradistinction to preaching "ought not to propose to itself to declare the fullness of revelation". It is no doubt also true that, once this specific understanding of theology is accepted, there can be little further objection to the theology of demythologization. Hence the question that remains is whether this specific understanding of theology is right and appropriate to the object.

I maintain that this is not the case, that rather both theological tradition and the object itself, on closer consideration, suggest to us that we should entertain exactly the opposite understanding of the task of theology.[1] Hence dogmatics

[1] This might be demonstrated indirectly on philosophical lines: for Martin Heidegger, the crowning witness of the Bultmann school, develops, if one considers the essential lineaments and the real interest of his thought, a philosophy of thinking which supports, indeed promotes, this opposite understanding of the task of theology. For Heidegger, the essence of original, essential, i.e. non-metaphysical, non-subjective thought, consists in existential encounter, or more precisely is only possible as existential encounter. Thinking is the basic action of man. It has the character of experience. For Bultmann and Fuchs, on the other hand, only faith itself is existential encounter and only preaching itself is a discourse based on existential

and preaching flow into each other. In dogmatics one can and must preach also, in a certain sense, just as in preaching one can and must, in a certain sense, teach dogmatically also. A glance at the classical works of dogmatics is sufficient to show us that this understanding of the situation is in accord with the great tradition of dogmatics.

＊ It may be necessary to affirm that dogmatics is the conscience of preaching and and that preaching, again, is the heart and soul of dogmatics. In order to be able to preach at all well, the preacher must engage in dogmatic reflection; while the dogmatic theologian, in order to teach dogma well and truly, must realize that he works with the intention of preaching and must constantly bear in mind the mission of preaching, even though he himself does not have to mount the pulpit Sunday by Sunday. That preacher who proposed to be nothing other than a preacher and to leave dogmatic thinking to the specialist in dogma would be a bad preacher, a preacher without heart and conscience. And the dogmatist who proposed to be nothing other than a dogmatist and to leave to the pastor the concern with the practical task of church preaching would be a bad church teacher; he again would be a dogmatist without heart and soul and conscience. In former times the theological teachers of the Church were, to a far greater extent than at present, preachers also and

encounter. Theological thought on the contrary is a discourse about the possibility of encounter and is completely divorced from encounter itself. The objections which are felt towards the theses of Bultmann arising from this conception of theology spring, in the words of Fuchs, from "the confusion between doctrine and preaching or the life of faith". If on the contrary we take seriously Heidegger's conception of thought, then we attain without difficulty an understanding of theology which sees it as a process of thinking from the heart of experience; more particularly, from the existential encounter which is the life of faith, thinking which is itself encounter, in short "a thinking out of faith".

Hence we might indeed adduce Heidegger as the crowning philosophical witness for our thesis concerning the continuity of preaching and dogmatics (cf. my book, *Denken und Sein—Der Weg Martin Heideggers und der Weg der Theologie*, 1st edn. 1959). This, however, as we have said, would be merely an indirect, philosophical demonstration of our thesis concerning the continuity of preaching and dogmatics. In what follows it will be a question of demonstrating the thesis in substantially theological terms, i.e. dogmatically and homiletically (and from both points of view at the same time).

conversely (e.g. Luther! Calvin! Zwingli!). This state of affairs reflected the essential truth of the situation. In the years of his Göttingen professorship Karl Barth seriously considered whether he ought not to return to the pastoral office.[1] The separation between the duties of preaching and theological teaching is a purely practical technical division of labour.

We have maintained that theology exercises a churchly duty of supervision and guardianship. Dogmatics then may not desire to be anything other than a kind of norm for preaching. As such it may not attempt to change itself into something radically different. In accordance with its essential task, aim and churchly function, it must itself in a certain sense exercise a preaching office. Dogmatics turns its attention to the preacher. Its task is to instruct the preacher. But it cannot "prove" anything to the preacher. It possesses no esoteric means of knowledge, it has at its disposal no knowledge which it might reveal to astonished hearers and authoritatively impart. It enjoys no specific means of knowledge which those whom it would address do not also enjoy. Thus dogmatics for its part can only preach, address, persuade. Dogmatics is a preaching to preachers, a pastoral charge of those who find themselves in the difficult, extreme, readily assailable position of having themselves to proclaim the Word of God.

It turns its attention to the preacher not with the intention of training him for the fulfilment of his vocation, not with technical means of assistance in the accomplishment of the duties of his calling. This would not be appropriate to the truth of the situation. In such a way it is not possible to be "trained" for the fulfilling of just *this* "calling". Rather dogmatics has to exercise a real preaching and pastoral office, has to bring about a sort of initiation which does not simply impart to the preacher what he must then pass on to his congregation, but which conveys to him the truth, truth by which he himself can live. *This* truth can

[1] Cf. Barth's correspondence with Ed. Thurneysen in the Thurneysen Festschrift, *Gottesdienst und Menschendienst*, EVZ-Verlag, 1958, pp. 155ff.

only be mediated by preaching and pastoral concern (both being basically the same thing).

Thus far dogmatics as a teaching office has also, by the very necessity of its nature, the character of preaching. And the real problem of dogmatics should then be formulated: *how are we to preach to the preacher?*

But if such a task is appreciated and taken seriously, then it is just not possible any longer to maintain a sharp distinction between the two tasks of preaching and dogmatic thinking. In this case we can no longer view things in such a way as, for example, to set over against each other dogmatics as speculation about doctrine and preaching as communication which has a severely practical aim, or dogmatics as a formal equipment of basic principles for the understanding of the kerygma and preaching as a fulfilled kerygma. No longer may we then say such things as: "In preaching it is a different matter. . . ." or: "In dogmatics it is otherwise. . . ."[1]

### 3. *Reciprocal Influence of Preaching and Dogmatics*

Dogmatics always implies preaching also; preaching always implies dogmatics also. Nevertheless this thesis of ours affirming the continuity of the two and the fluidity of their boundary has not yet been substantiated. We have asserted and we have elucidated and illustrated the meaning of our assertion, but we have not yet proved—unless it be by means of the indirect and merely outlined proof through Heidegger, which, although no doubt convincing enough as far as the interpretation of Heidegger's own work is concerned, cannot be considered a decisive argument theologically. The true, direct and theologically quite convincing proof we shall only be able to produce in connexion with the object itself

---

[1] As was once the reply given me by an all-too-faithful pupil of Bultmann when I asked him—knowing well that the dimension of the "world" and among other things the doctrine of divine providence are imperilled in Bultmann's existentialist theology—how he would preach on the text of Matt. 10:29ff. (*Are not two sparrows sold for a penny? And not one of them will fall to the ground without your Father's will. But even the hairs of your head are all numbered. Fear not therefore. . . .*): "Well of course in preaching it's quite a different matter. I could no doubt preach about it. But preaching and theology are two quite different things. . . ."

*in concreto,* by conclusively showing the continuity of preaching and dogmatics in individual cases of particular dogmatic problems and over the widest possible field.

The fact of continuity presupposed, the question immediately arises: of what nature is this continuity and how does it specifically find expression from the angle of preaching and doctrine? Moreover, even though we accept the continuity of the two spheres as a necessary mode of their relationship, we shall not just simply equate them and leave out of account their real difference. The theological teacher does not in fact do precisely the same thing as the preacher does in the pulpit; or at least he does the same thing in a different way. Hence there certainly remains, even within the framework of this presupposed continuity, the question as to the characteristic *difference* between preaching and dogmatics. What is the line of demarcation between them? And even though it be a fluid line, how are the two spheres to be characterized which thus flow into each other?

With this question we have pierced to the heart of the crucial problem. Hence again we shall here be concerned to illuminate this line of demarcation by reference to particular dogmatic problems. We must ask the question: *How does the preacher's task with its urgency lead to dogmatic questioning and formulation?* We must attempt to show how far, in detail, the path of the kerygma which proceeds from scripture through dogmatic questioning and formulation to emerge in preaching is no unnecessarily circuitous route. We shall show rather how far dogmatics is necessary for the sake of preaching and that there must be this "reflective function of preaching itself". We must attempt to show how far and in what way the one and indivisible kerygma, the primal fact of preaching as of theology, the revealing encounter with the living God in His Word, is reflected both in preaching and in dogmatic work, and how these reflections mutually condition and enhance each other. If we succeed in demonstrating this reciprocal effect by reference to individual instances of particular dogmatic formulation and of the preacher's message which in such formulation is crystallized into doctrine, then we shall have both demonstrated the continuity which we have asserted and also have ascertained the boundary which divides preaching from dogmatics.

In further pursuing the inquiry in which we have already become engaged through this concrete posing of the problem, we shall no doubt gain various general insights, that is to say, insights which can be verified along the whole line of the nexus between preaching and dogmatics. These insights we may now foreshadow in some small degree.

We shall expect for example to come up against this fact, namely that behind every particular sermon that is preached there stands and is afresh disclosed the dogmatic consideration of the unity, the wholeness, the truth and the intelligible coherence of the kerygma. I can never preach about everything; it is not right that I should wish to express "everything". We preach in antitheses: sometimes of the judgment, sometimes of the mercy of God, sometimes of the cross, sometimes of the resurrection, sometimes of justification, sometimes of sanctification. As preachers, we testify to God's honour and glory in a one-sided way, concentrating our attention on the particular aspect which the text suggests to our minds. If it is given us to testify truly in this way, then God is present as the one, eternal, unchanging being, and the particular sermon enfolds, in all its particularity, the whole. It is the precise concern of dogmatics to consider this whole. And thus the oneness and wholeness of the necessarily one-sided particular sermon is conclusively shown as it is reflected in dogmatic thought. We utter what is particular and fragmentary, but by reflecting upon it dogmatically, we endeavour to think our way through to the sustaining whole.

No doubt in this task we shall always remain seekers after something that exceeds our grasp, for it is reserved to God alone to bestow upon the Church, through the sacrament of the word, the wholeness of His undivided presence. Here lies the frontier, not only of preaching, but also of dogmatics. But the attempt at least, in the particular and from the particular, to think out the whole, remains the task of

26

dogmatics and, by implication, the task of the preacher also. The particular sermon is like the smaller part of the iceberg that is visible above the water; the rest, the totality of the kerygma committed to the Church, floats sustainingly beneath the surface of the water. This symbolizes dogmatic reflection on the wholeness of the doctrine which sustains and enfolds the particular sermon. We ought to feel uneasy about those critics who declare that they "miss" references to the "cross" or the "resurrection" in some particular sermon. As though it were the duty of the preacher to be always expressing everything! As though it were his duty at any and every cost to push into his sermon every article of Christian doctrine! For where the cross is truly proclaimed, then the resurrection is proclaimed also; where God's grace is preached, so is also His judgment; where justification is truly declared, so also is the process of sanctification.

A further general insight, which we shall presumably attain in pursuing particular investigations, concerns the manner in which preaching affects dogmatic work. Preaching is the impulse of power which drives the thinker to his dogmatic work, it is the element or the medium within which dogmatic principles as such are alone at all possible, it is the inspiration which urges the theologian to think out to the true conclusion his dogmatic sequences of thought, which compels him to the building up of a dogmatic system, and thus finally it is the criterion by which the validity of doctrine is to be measured.

For example, we are confronted by a Biblical text such as the passage in Genesis 3 relating the fall of man, so meaningful in dogmatic tradition; and we ask ourselves whether and how, on the basis of this text, there can be framed dogmatic teaching about sin. The motive behind this question concerning dogma is however the need to pierce to the clear and responsible teaching implicit in scripture, and this need arises from the exigencies of the preaching mission of the Church. How may we, how ought we, to preach about sin? What word of the preacher will in this matter be clear, convincing, fully responsible? The preacher can only *per nefas*, with guilt, elude the dogmatic questioning. On the other hand, there may not be any immanently isolated, self-evolved dogmatic system which by-passes the living needs of the preacher. Thus dogmatic teaching about sin and the fall is again to be measured by the yardstick of the preacher's task, and the question will be: "Can such doctrine be preached?" Hence dogmatic teaching will be disclosed as bad dogmatic teaching, if it is shown to be inadequate to the mission of preaching. We are faced then by the fact of reciprocal action: doctrine grows from the task of preaching incumbent upon the Church, and the "needs" which this involves, and in turn it operates in a regulative way upon the actual fulfilment of this preaching mission.[1] Thus preaching is at one and the same time an impulse of power and a criterion, and is itself both impelled and criticized by dogma.

### 4. *The Heidelberg Catechism as a Basic Text*

In order to study in some detail the relation and the reciprocal influences of dogmatics and preaching, it will be helpful to take a certain document as a guide. In principle, any essential dogmatic work could perform the same service for us. We might think for example of the *Church Dogmatics* or of other dogmatic writings of Karl Barth, who is certainly fully aware throughout the whole scope of his teaching of the constitutive reciprocal relation of dogmatics and preaching, in spite of the fact that he does not stress it so specifically as a guide, a method and a point of view as we intend deliberately to do in what follows. Our own choice has fallen on the Heidelberg Catechism and in particular on its

[1] The fact that dogmatics should be suitable to the "needs" of the preacher does not of course mean in our context of thought a muzzling of theory by practice, in the sense of an unwholesome utilitarianism or an ignorant pietism, nor does it imply that we are disallowing the so-called "intellectual honesty" of theology which is rightly so much claimed. That preaching should become a criterion for doctrine sets in fact no limits to the severely honest and in the truest sense scientific thinking of the theologian, but on the contrary emancipates it. For the most inward and objective need of the preacher is precisely that he should grasp the word of scripture in its clarity and responsibility. How could we serve the Lord in any other way than by uprightness and sincerity?

doctrine of sin, since this text seems to us especially adapted for such an undertaking both because of its obviously doctrinal and its obviously practical and kerygmatic character.

The Heidelberg Catechism was issued by the Elector Frederick III on November 15, 1563, and was decreed to be a valid church order throughout the Palatinate. It is an integral part of the whole church liturgy, where it occupies a position between the formularies for baptism and those for the Lord's Supper. Its authors were the two theologians Zacharias Ursinus and Kaspar Olevianus, aged respectively 28 and 26. Henry Bullinger assessed the work in the year of its appearance in the following terms: *"Plana sunt omnia, piissima, fructuosissima; succincta brevitate comprehendentia magnas res et copias. . . ."* (Could there be a better witness to a theological product?) *". . . Arbitror meliorem Catechismus editum non esse.* DEO *sit gloria, qui largiatur successum!"*[1] The famous Question 80 which deals with the difference between the Christian Lord's Supper and the papist Mass (regarded as a work of "accursed idolatry") was first included in the 2nd edition and was perhaps personally written by the Elector Palatine himself.

In the words of the church order to which it belongs, this Catechism has a fourfold purpose: to serve for the instruction of youth, to provide a standard of belief for clergy and teachers, to be read in church worship as part of the liturgy, and finally to lay down basic themes for the afternoon sermons on the 52 Sundays of the year. Thus the same text exercises a catechetical, a theological, a liturgical and a kerygmatic function!

In its structure this Catechism occupies a position intermediate between the catechisms of Luther and Calvin. With Calvin and unlike Luther it treats the decalogue after the Apostolicum; hence it places the law, regarded as the *tertius usus legis*, after the Gospel. But alongside this feature—and in this respect the structure follows the lines of the Lutheran

[1] "Everything is clearly expressed, deeply devotional, likely to produce rich spiritual growth, dealing with vast themes and a wealth of material in a concise pithy style. In my opinion, no better Catechism has been published. To GOD be the glory, and may He grant success!"

catechism—the law, regarded as the *usus elenchticus*, receives
expression in the form of the twofold commandment (Qu. 4),
and in this capacity comes before the Apostolicum. Thus in
general terms the mediatory, the irenic note, the emphasis
on what is common to all evangelical Christianity, is characteristic of our Catechism. The "reformed" doctrines in the
narrower sense are really to be found only in Questions 47–48
which consider the mode of omnipresence of the exalted
Lord, and in Questions 75–79, which treat of the mode of
the real presence of Christ in the elements of the Lord's
Supper.

This Catechism has rightly been described as the "work of
the second generation". Gottfried W. Locher in the *Evan-
gelische Theologie* has in this sense given a very fine charac-
terization of the Heidelberg Catechism, of its historical
setting, its attitude and its influence:

> The Heidelberg Catechism is one of the ripest fruits of the
> reformation movement, and a summing up of its net results.
> Although it was produced in the midst of urgent disputes, and
> in the shadow of the emerging Counter-Reformation, it breathes
> in every line the spirit of peace, confidence and even cheerful-
> ness. Its systematization and the consistent thoroughness of
> its thought remind one already of the period of orthodoxy
> which was about to dawn and which no doubt it helped to
> introduce. At the same time its unflinching aim to secure the
> life of personal faith and sanctification in its treatment of
> every particle of doctrine assimilated the emphases of the
> Anabaptist circles which were especially active in the Pala-
> tinate. In this way it influenced puritanism with its turning
> towards self-examination, while along with the third book of
> Calvin's *Institutes* it exerted the deepest influence on the
> movement of pietism, at the cradle of which it stood. This
> fact attests its irenic character still more strongly than does
> its complete renunciation of polemics. The common evangelical
> spirit breaks through decisively in the stress on the substi-
> tutionary doctrine of the atonement and in the central place
> it accords to the doctrine of justification. . . .
>
> All in all, it is a work of the second generation. The striving
> for new insights has here been freed from the spirit of punc-
> tilious instruction, at a time when the terrors of persecution

were already weighing on the Church. Thus this Catechism became not merely a book of doctrine or a confession of faith, but truly a book of consolation. This means that it is a book of meditation and of prayer from its first line to its last, and as such has proved its worth a thousand times (*Ev. Theol.* 1957, Vol. 12).

The study of it which follows is meant to be a *conversation* bearing constantly in mind the basic themes common to all theology, and thus far it will be a genuine conversation, not a historian's examination of the work! While taking seriously the work and its authors as our conversational partners in the great *communio sanctorum*, we shall not avoid criticizing the Catechism and measuring its formulations by the yardstick of our present-day theological insights. Broadly speaking our criticism of the Catechism will be especially directed, firstly to its too verbal understanding of scripture, and secondly (a point which coheres with the first) to its too narrow conception, on the lines of a purely historical saving process, of that event which takes place between God and man. This difference of outlook will be acutely felt in the course of the dogmatic passages of thought which follow, especially when we come to discuss the fall and original sin. Apart from this, however, the Catechism contains, both in its sequences of thought and its great insights and particular formulations, enough of the most genuine theological and kerygmatic expression of Christian self awareness, enough cogent and convincing and clear words, as to make it valid, assimilable, and of benefit to us today.

Theses developed in Chapter 1.

1. Theology is necessary for the sake of preaching. It exercises a supervisory office with regard to the Church's gospel proclamation, for it concerns itself with the themes that are to be preached. Dogmatics as the highest stage of theological reflection may be defined as the reflective aspect of preaching itself.
2. There is a continuity between preaching and dogmatics. The latter is implicitly preaching also and preaching in itself implies dogmatics. Dogmatics may be described as preaching to the preacher. This point of view disallows the programme of theology

set today by the school of Bultmann, which understands preaching and doctrine, in spite of their belonging together, as two sharply distinct activities.

3. Although the frontier between preaching and dogmatics is fluid, the distinction between them is not simply cancelled. The difference between, and the mutual influences exercised by, these two spheres must be studied with reference to particular dogmatic problems. For this purpose the Heidelberg Catechism is eminently suitable, since it is clearly both a dogmatic and kerygmatic work of striking brevity and terseness.

4. A consideration of preaching shows that it is at once the impulsive power and the criterion of dogmatic work and also the medium within which the formulation of doctrine becomes possible.

# CHAPTER 2

## DOGMATICS AND PREACHING AS THE UNFOLDING OF THE ONE KERYGMA

(Heidelberg Catechism, Questions 1 and 2.)

Question 1. "What is your one comfort and trust in living and dying?

"That in body and soul, in life and death, I am not my own, but belong to my faithful Redeemer Jesus Christ who with His dear blood has fully paid the ransom price for all my sins and has delivered me from the power of the devil, and who therefore has me in His keeping, in such wise that without the will of my Father in heaven not a hair of my head can fall, and that in fact everything must serve for my blessedness. Therefore He also assures me of eternal life through the outpouring of His Holy Spirit upon me and makes me heartily willing and ready to live henceforth to Him."

Question 2. "What points of doctrine must you know in order to live and die happily in this faith?

"Three points: Firstly, how great is my sin and misery; secondly how I am saved from all my sins and misery; and thirdly how thankful I must be to God for such salvation."

THESE TWO questions and answers form the opening of the Heidelberg Catechism. They relate to the whole of what follows and as it were contain in themselves this whole. Hence—in order at once to grasp the transition from the text of the Catechism to the special object of our enquiry—on the basis of this opening we shall have to ponder the whole: the unity of the proclamation on the one hand, and the unity of the dogma on the other. Question 1 relates to the whole in a material manner, Question 2 rather in a formal manner: this principle of division governs the whole writing. Yet both stand in the closest relation to each other, as the text shows. The one flows from the other. Question 2 specifies the articles of doctrine which must be known in order to live and die happily in the faith described in Question 1, i.e. in order to embody that faith in actual life. Question 2 gives the formal principle for the manifestation of what Question 1 substantially contains. Thus in the framework of our inquiry we suppose that Question 1 will relate to the content, Question 2 to the formal structure of dogmatics and preaching as a whole.

### 1. *The Unity of Preaching and the Unity of Dogmatics*

In his excellent study of "Prayer in the Reformation sense and in the light of the Heidelberg Catechism" (*"Das Vornehmste Stuck der Dankbarkeit"*, *Ev. Theologie*, I, 1957, Vol. 12) Gottfried Locher says with regard to the sequence of thought in the catechism: "Questions 2 to 129 are nothing other than developments and substantiations of the one trust in life and death which Question 1 puts before us" (p. 565). This formula is more precise and appropriate than some simple statement such as that Question 1 sums up the contents of the Catechism in advance. It would be still more correct to formulate with Karl Barth (*Die Christliche Lehre nach dem Heidelberger Katechismus*, 1948): "Question 1 puts this faith in a nutshell and seeks in one sentence to say what the faith is that can give such assurance" (p. 23). Perhaps in fact Question 1 is already an unfolding rather than a summary. The one is not the summary of the many (Qu. 2–129) but the many is an unfolding of the one. Hence we must think on the basis of the one, which in this case is the short declaration of Question 1, which again is perhaps an unfolding, an unfolding of something still more terse, something still more "one", something that is probably no longer to be expressed in words, namely the comfort of faith itself—a comfort consisting in the sovereign presence of just *this* Lord and God.

In the movement of the development of the one into the many, thus disclosed, we recognize the structural principle of both dogmatics and preaching—a structural principle which is higher than that suggested by Question 2, for the latter intimates merely the mode in which the one is developed. Because they are a multiplicity of words and sentences developed from the one, and legitimate only as such a development and articulation, both preaching and dogmatics form a unity and this unity which they unfold and manifest is in both cases the same. It is only the manner, the style of the development and articulation which is characteristically different.The aim of the articulation is also different, in that the dogmatic explication is intended to be of use through its clarification of the total context of that "existential", "applied" development which is to be found in preaching. But the unity of dogmatics corresponds to the unity of preaching and both gain their unity because they are in equal measure, if not absolutely in the same way, an articulation of the one and the same, of that which is ultimately inexpressible, of that which exists before all human words, be they words of dogmatics or words of preaching, of that effectual Reality which is prior to all human speech. This ultimate Reality is the one God, the one Lord, the one faith! And thus from our insight into this underlying oneness of the object we are led to appreciate the continuity between dogmatics and preaching.

This unity and wholeness which are constituted by the articulation of the one may especially clearly be understood with reference to dogmatics and its specific programme. There is one God, one Lord and one faith: this is the foundation fact of dogmatics, and in all circumstances it must hold fast to this. It may not split up its one object into multiple "objects of faith" nor must it allow its doctrine to be dissipated in various "articles of belief". Rather the oneness of the sole object of faith is to be preserved. To the oneness of the *fides qua creditur*, of the one indivisible act of faith which lies beyond our control, there corresponds the oneness of the *fides quae creditur* which is announced in the discourse of proclamation and dogmatics and must not be betrayed through them. Indeed it would be even more correct to formulate the matter conversely: to the oneness of the *fides quae creditur* there corresponds the oneness of the *fides qua creditur*, and though this latter may become ambivalent from an empirical point of view, problematic in its exposure to attack on the psychological level, and questionable as regards its integrality, yet it remains spanned and held by the transcendent unambiguous oneness of the object of faith. For the object of faith is of course in the last analysis not some doctrine or other, nor even some confession of faith or kerygma, but God Himself as He who stands over against faith.[1]

This indissoluble unity is the very principle of dogmatics and of theology in general, the one principle that must be understood if the essence of theology is to be understood. For the theologian there are not certain things which are to be believed and other things which are also to be believed, so that the sum total of things to be believed would look like an arithmetical sum to which and from which additions and subtractions might be proposed. This may well be the current conception of dogmatics, but it springs from an utterly false idea of the essential character of dogmatics. Nor has that character to do with a plurality of so-called "saving facts", which are to be believed primarily as a whole or, if not, in part (for instance with the elimination of the Virgin Birth or such like) and then as the sum total of what is believed made to cohere with each other by systematic thought. None of this really hits the mark. We do not believe saving facts but we believe in God (*Credimus in Deum*— and that means also and primarily *credimus Deo*, i.e. "we trust in God").

This faith is one and indivisible, just as God Himself, to whom man in faith commits himself, is one and indivisible. And what are commonly called "saving facts" have meaning only when understood as an integrating, meaningful phase of man's encounter with God who is one and indivisible; that is, man's encounter with God as the One, who has made

[1] The relation of confrontation and the object are thus the same. We might also use the idea of the "thing" which Karl Barth particularly likes. We do not agree with the current widespread attitude of denouncing the conception of the "object". But our thought is not in consequence "objectivizing".

and sustains the world, who has become man, who was crucified and rose again, who reigns in majesty and will return. All these phases, all these relations to the world as a whole, our sin, our death, our future and that of the world, and so on, are included in the meaning of that act of faith which is a relationship to the living God. This relationship would not be what it is, God would be other than what He in fact (for us) is, He would be estranged from Himself, if any one of these relations were lacking.

Faith is no empty "mere attitude" of man, lacking in concrete content; it implies and includes all these phases of relationship. Hence it is not a question of subtraction or addition, it is a question of the *character* of the whole and indivisibly one. In every single one of those phases the whole is at stake; in every single one, the whole is represented. In saying all this, we do not mean to assert that anything of what is usually reckoned among the "saving facts" did not happen. In the point of view we are putting forward there does not take place an evaporation of history into the "idea", a dissolution into the conception of a timeless "quality of God". We are merely asserting that theology ought not to proceed from the belief in the factuality of such "saving facts". This would be meaningless and contrary to the essence of the thing. Theology is only theology when it holds directly in view the living God who of course integrates all those phases in the way that has been described. Thus it is what it ought to be: an explication of faith as a relation of confrontation with the one God.

Moreover what in this context of thought is the meaning of "truly happened"?—if indeed it is proposed to discuss the real factuality of "saving facts". What yardstick do we apply when we wish to make a statement about the real factuality of the "saving facts"? Are we not tempted in such a matter to measure the reality of God by the criterion of an unclarified and unproved idea of "historical factuality", without taking into account the fact that creation, incarnation, crucifixion and resurrection, ascension and second coming move on quite another plane of "happening" and belong to a quite different dimension of divine history and cosmic relevance? Not that we would wish to suggest by this the construction of a dualism (which in the last resort would be docetic) between "history" and "super-history". We simply leave the question open and do not imagine that we already know, precisely and in normative fashion, what history is, in such wise as to be able to derive from our knowledge a criterion by which to assess the dimensions in which divine revelation moves. Nothing is thereby altered in the confession *"vere Deus—vere homo"* (truly God and truly man).

We have a certain, if inadequate, illustration of our thesis that the so-called "saving facts" are not single facts to be established as such, but integrating meaningful phases in the whole indivisible divine relationship to the world, when we consider the character of personal encounter between human beings. In my relationship to some other human being the past that we have in common, with its particular stages, its essential events, forms an integral part. The relation between us in the present would not be just *this* relation without *that* past. Of course we may gain an approach to those events apart from our own relationship, to some extent an objective, "impersonal" approach, inasmuch as perhaps there were other persons with us at the time who might be in a position to report the events from their own points of view (again differing from each other) so that by means of comparison something like an "objective picture" could emerge. (Real pure objectivity does not of course arise even then; it is in fact unattainable by men, and there is occasion for a thesis maintaining that it does not exist at all, that rather all historical reality is and remains by its very nature a matter of appearance.)[1] As regards encounter with God, the position is on the other hand that we gain access to the integrating historical moments, the so-called "saving facts", solely through personal encounter itself, solely through faith. Creation, incarnation, resurrection, ascension, can in no

---

[1] Cf. my essay "Die Frage nach dem historischen Jesus und die Ontologie der Geschichte", EVZ-Verlag, *Theol. Studien*, 62, 1960.

way be ascertained as pure historical facts; they disclose their reality only in their meaningfulness for faith.

In this sense therefore the attack led today by Bultmann's school against the idea and the theology of saving facts is thoroughly to be supported. Of course in Bultmann's language it is not a question of encounter with God but of self-understanding. Yet the two ideas are related to each other and what is conveyed by them could in fact be the same thing. And in *this* particular matter, both Bultmann and ourselves are concerned to stress the same point: we are concerned to set aside the false shock of the gospel, which results from the suggestion that the individual facts of salvation require specific assent, in order to let shine more brightly the true scandal of the gospel which is its challenge that I must decide for God.

Thus the unity of dogmatics, its character as the explication of the one, becomes apparent from Question 1 of the Heidelberg Catechism and its relation to the 128 questions that follow, if indeed it is true that, in the Catechism as a whole, what is involved is only the amplification of the faith contained in Question 1. The same now applies to preaching. Preaching too has to do always with the one and the single. Our preaching does not communicate this, that and the other, it proclaims always and only the one self-same thing, the "one comfort in life and in death," and this proclamation of the one essential truth must ring through all its communications, its counsels, its challenges, its judgments, and embody itself in them, otherwise they are not stamped with the character of preaching. Preaching has always the same content, but this content cannot be expressed once for all in an unambiguous communication; it expresses itself truly but never with final validity and adequacy in an unlimited number of particular sermons. We preach, not a multiplicity of various things, which are "to be believed", but we preach the one God. "I believe, and so I speak" (2 Cor. 4:13); the oneness of the proclamation corresponds to the oneness of faith and so, as we have already seen, to the oneness of God. And to extend this line of thought still further we might say: to the oneness of the proclamation corresponds the oneness of dogmatics. In the many texts of the Bible and so, as is right, in the sermons which are preached about them, the one whole unbroken gospel is mirrored.

Thus we deduce from Question 1 of the Catechism first the structural similarity, the nexus between preaching and dogmatics. Then also and from the same source we infer their continuity. For when we say that the unified structure of dogmatics corresponds to that of proclamation, and this not only formally but also substantially, since the one thing to be unfolded is in both cases the same; when we further assert that dogmatics, because it has to serve preaching, must have the same structure as the latter, then the continuity of the two appears, as we affirmed at the outset, inevitable. The manifest structural relationship of the two spheres, deducible from Question 1, is an argument for their continuity.

This structural relationship serves us then as a first general argument for our thesis. But precisely in view of this situation there should become apparent a further general viewpoint regarding the difference between preaching and dogmatics. We note that it is the special characteristic of dogmatics that it is concerned with the understanding of the whole, with systematization, whereas preaching is not. Preaching on the other hand is marked by its bent towards the *hic et nunc*, the here and now, its concern with a given pastoral situation. This trait is completely foreign to dogmatics. Pastoral situations are numberless and cannot be summarized in a synoptic view; the sermons to be addressed to them are also numberless. Church proclamation is an unfolding of the one and the whole in such wise that it unfolds it *ad hoc*, that is to say, in relation to a particular text of the Bible and in addressing itself to a specific pastoral situation.

The individual sermon is self-enclosed; it looks neither to the right nor to the left; it says what it is bidden to say under a specific necessity (that arising from the text and the immediate situation). It does not need to produce any total context, to engender any system of thought; for the concrete address to an immediate situation needs no system (excepting of course the sequence of the thoughts, the arrangement of ideas in the particular sermon). On the other hand, dogmatics unfolds the one and the whole in a systematic manner, with constant regard to the total context. Not that dogmatics could only be expounded with reference to the system as a whole. It is certainly very possible to investigate particular dogmatic questions. But its bent towards systematization does not consist merely in its concern with the totality; it also always characterizes the individual passage of thought. The particular dogmatic passage of thought, indeed dogmatic thinking in general, has as an intrinsic characteristic the tendency towards systematization. In thinking thus, the dogmatist is well aware that he cannot drink up the sea, that he cannot enfold the mystery of God within any system. The system is our own system, not God's, who needs no system because He is the truth itself. But we dogmatists are called to strive to reach a system, to think in view of the whole, so that we may be in a position to answer for the particular thing that we assert.

The particular truth can only be guaranteed in our thinking when we pay attention to its total context and bear in mind all the possibilities of thought which arise in connexion with the special thing about which we are concerned. This the sermon does not need to do and ought not as a rule to do, because it is limited to a special aim, and attuned to the *hic et nunc* of the concrete situation to which it is addressed. In the sermon, considerations of the systematic whole appear as a rule to be tedious padding. But dogmatics has to take upon itself this very task of systematization. It must deliberately maintain its tendency to think in terms of a system of thought, and even when it is dealing with the particular, it must see it expressly in the context of a whole perhaps never before postulated. Thus for example in investigating some eucharistic problem the dogmatist must needs take into account the manifest connexions with Christology, ecclesiology and eschatology. And it is on this tendency to think in terms of the whole, on this systematic work of the dogmatist that the individual sermon rests for support. It is from this source that it wins its spiritual vitality. (Technically speaking! For essentially the preacher gains spiritual vitality only from his awareness of the forgiveness of his sins!)

Thus we see the difference between proclamation and dogmatics to consist in the way in which they develop the one. It should be said further, with reference to the systematic development which is characteristic of dogmatics, that of course there can here be no question of any synthetic systematization stemming from an attempt to proceed from below upwards, from the many to the one. For, as we have seen, there must always be an unfolding of the one: hence the one and not the many is the presupposition lying behind systematic work. Even the multiplicity of the Biblical texts, with which dogmatics has to be concerned, is not a genuine multiplicity but merely the manifold reflection of the one and the same truth. For the theological relevance of the multiple Biblical texts is an effect of the one faith; and this faith is faith no doubt through the mediation of the many texts of the Bible, but only because through this manifoldness it is the one God who is looking at us. Thus dogmatics as a whole has an analytic character. Every dogmatic sentence is analytical in that its predicate is already implicit in the common subject of all dogmatic sentences, namely in the one truth that is to be amplified. Preaching cannot add anything to the oneness of this truth; no more can dogmatics.

## 2. *The Text of the First Question and Answer*

The one truth is properly the inexpressible (by men): it is the *verbum efficax Dei*, the effective word of God. In order however that proclamation and dogmatics may become aware of their ground, dogmatics is permitted to attempt to name the one from which all else flows. Because it is essentially the inexpressible, various names are possible. The shortest and most pregnant may well be that which consists in the two-word statement *Kyrios Christos*, Christ is Lord. The Heidelberg Catechism has found an appropriate and striking description of the one truth in the framing of Question 1. The answer consists of a single sentence, probably intentionally. (We are also thinking here of the explanations of the three articles of the confession of faith in Luther's short catechism, each one of which is contained in a single artistically moulded sentence.) In this connexion the syntactic form is intended to underline and bring home the unity of the object.

It becomes clear from the wording of the text that what is here in question is not "saving facts", but the "one comfort in life and death", that is to say, an existential event which happens to me: the fact that I have a source of comfort, a standing-ground, an assurance, a security, and a hope. Yet in connexion with this question about a (as it were) subjective reality, about "my comfort", we are immediately referred back to the reality of God *extra nos*, outside ourselves. Karl Barth rightly stresses in his comments on the Heidelberg Catechism that the "decisive little sentence in the long period which forms the first answer is: I belong to Jesus Christ. All the rest is only an explanation of these five words. About man there is only this to be said, namely, that he belongs totally to Jesus Christ, with body and soul, in life and in death. He is the property of Jesus Christ, without limit and without reservation . . ." (*op. cit.* p. 24). Thus within the description of the one original ultimate reality we have once again a nucleus and its expansion. The nucleus, that is, the words "I belong to Jesus Christ", affirms moreover exactly the same thing as the primitive Christian confession *Kyrios Christos*. I have been taken away from the autonomy of myself; I am not my own Lord and master, I have not the power of disposal over myself. Another has the disposal of me: to Him I belong. I am His *doulos*, His slave.

It is just this situation which is deliberately underlined by the little words: "not my own". I find through that

Other a limit to my existence; in Him my existence is grounded. In Him I find my own true transcendence—a word which signifies also the Other, the One who both limits and sustains. And this transcendence is not an empty abstraction, not a mere limitation constructed and postulated in terms of human life. It is a concrete reality, it is this living Other, in whose power and under whose authoritative disposal I am situated. And it is just this situation, the fact that I have a transcendence, and a transcendence of this nature, the fact that I am not my own, that I have been removed from my self-dominion, that I am not the master of my life—it is this that constitutes my true and only comfort in living and dying. For if we presuppose the contrary, if I am my own lord and master, if I have the complete control of myself, then I have no comfort, no ground of confidence; for I can never settle the issue of life and death by myself. I can neither escape from life into death, nor can I escape from death into life. Both equally threaten me. I can neither rescue myself by dying from the menacing senselessness of life, nor can I save myself from the menacing senselessness of death by living. In that case, I am delivered over to nothingness both in life and in death. Paradoxically my true standing-ground and security lies in the fact that I am removed from the mastery of myself.

This is an elemental situation, so elemental that it cannot be further explained. The only approximating analogy is the one which determines the language of the New Testament and which obviously also lies behind the thought in our Question 1, namely the analogy of the *Kyrios-doulos*, the master-slave relationship as constituted by ancient law. But the situation of not belonging to oneself, of being delivered from self-dominion, with which we are here concerned, applies not to some particular group of men, but to all men. For that very reason it is impalpable and intangible. It is a basic situation, which demands a basic decision. It is just as elemental and irreducible (or rather more so) as the personal being of man, and his responsibility. But like the latter it can be proclaimed and understood as a claim. It is this very proclamation and claim which is the heart and essence of all preaching. Through all that we communicate in our sermons, through all our exhortation and challenges, there sound this proclamation and this claim. All that we say in preaching is a development of it. Here lies the real kerygma of Christian preaching. And whatever preaching may demand of the hearer is only a concrete embodiment of this basic decision.

The Other, to whom I am surrendered, is called Jesus Christ. He does not need to be pictured to us. He does not need to be defined, distinguished and described in His qualities, so that we may be able to identify Him. He is as elemental as the kerygma itself, as the claim expressed by all preaching, as the basic situation in which we are removed from self-dominion. For this basic situation only exists at all for His sake. Jesus is just this: namely, the Lord of our being. No more need be said to enable us to know who He is. No doubt it has already become clear that in our argument up to the present, in talking about the kerygma, about the situation in which we are removed from self-dominion, about its proclamation and the claim it implies, we have been following the existential theology of Bultmann. But now, following the Heidelberg Catechism, it is equally plain that we have deviated from Bultmann's line of thought, for we have now to do with Jesus Christ Himself, with Jesus Christ in person. He Himself, His Person, is the essential ground of the deliverance from self which the kerygma proclaims.

The concrete reality of the Person of Jesus Christ is already fully contained in the affirmation that I am His, "with body and soul, in life and in death". I can understand the meaning of my life through the belief that I am not my own, I am His. And I am bidden to understand myself so. Thus far we follow Bultmann. But we think that we must go beyond him, by saying that such self-understanding necessarily contains a personal relationship to the Person of Jesus Christ the Lord.

Yet in Question 1 the Person of Jesus Christ is made known in one specific way, namely through the reference to

45

the event of the cross. This is the only moment in the life of Jesus Christ which is here purposely referred to: "who with His dear blood has fully paid the ransom price for all my sins and has delivered me from the power of the devil". Obviously this event is regarded as especially meaningful in connexion with a basic statement of the personal attributes of Jesus Christ. Only in later contexts of the Catechism do we find mentioned the other Christological themes. But the cross stands already enshrined at the heart of Question 1 and clearly with the idea of laying a foundation for the momentous statement contained in those five words: "I belong to Jesus Christ". Jesus is the owner of my life because for me He is the Crucified. The authors of the Catechism are obviously here thinking of the relation of the slave to his purchaser and owner, hence of the New Testament ἀπολύτρωσις theory as an interpretation of the cross. In the later questions and answers however which deal with the cross the thought of the ἀπολύτρωσις plays no further part; it is rather the satisfaction theory of Anselm which is in control. This shows that in Question 1 also it is only the allusion to the cross itself which is important. The thought of the purchase price is there only incidentally and no special significance is ascribed to it.

The mention of the cross as an explanation of the basic and decisive affirmation of the text points outwards in two ways, pointing away from that self-understanding which constitutes my sole comfort. Firstly it points us to the historical man Jesus of Nazareth crucified under Pontius Pilate. Next, it immediately refers us from our own life-experience to that of Jesus Christ Himself. The source of my "subjective" trust lies in an "objective" situation; as the one who has such comfort and trust I realize myself to be implicated in the experience of Jesus Christ Himself. In fact we must say that in this text, which is concerned with my sole comfort in living and dying, it is not only my existence but that of Jesus Christ Himself which is at stake. For my sole comfort and the fact that I belong to Jesus Christ consist in this—namely that He has staked His life for me and with His own existence has substituted Himself for me. In the view of the Heidelberg Catechism this fact alone makes possible the decisive statement about my comfort springing from the fact that I belong to Jesus Christ. This brings fully into our view the "dimension of Jesus Christ Himself" which in Bultmann's interpretation of the saving event threatens to vanish.

From a homiletic standpoint the reference to the cross in Question 1 undoubtedly signifies this: that inasmuch as we preach this claim, and declare the kerygma of being delivered from one's self (and thereby being given back to one's self) we are preaching at the same time the Person of the Lord Jesus Christ. The Person of Jesus Christ Himself and thus His honour and glorification form an integral part of the proclamation of this divine claim.

If now we analyse the nucleus of our text into its dogmatic elements, we note the following themes: first, that of the cross ("who with His dear blood . . .) then that of divine providence ("and who therefore has me in His keeping in such wise that without the will of my Father . . .), and thirdly the *testimonium Spiritus Sancti* in connexion with (*a*) the hope of eternal life ("assures me of eternal life through the outpouring of His Holy Spirit") and (*b*) the theme of the Christian way of life ("living henceforth to Him"). As we have seen, the reference to the cross occupies a quite special place. In the remaining three elements the fundamental affirmation of the text is amplified and explained. And this not dogmatically—for the dogmatic explanation is to be found in Questions 2 to 129—but in a more personal and direct way, i.e. in a *kerygmatic-existential* way.

The comfort which is meant and specified here means for us the plain security of being in the Father's keeping, the assured hope of eternal life and the obligation, the sharp challenge, to adopt a certain way of life. The entire context of our personal life, our living and dying, within which we need this sole comfort and trust, comes here into the foreground: our everyday life and fortunes, in every detail of which we know ourselves to be surrendered to the almighty

God, the Father of our Lord Jesus Christ, and kept secure by Him; our temporal future which up to a certain point we can fashion by our own planning (this implies the question of ethics); the more general demand, "to live henceforth to Him"; finally the frontier of death to which we are hastening with our everyday life and fortunes, our hopes and plans, and beyond which we have nothing to expect except the Lord Himself. This Question 1 is a compact and pregnant designation of the one and the total reality which in the catechism as a whole is amplified. Question 1 itself has a kerygmatic rather than a dogmatic character. The dogmatic motives which have become visible in it provide less a starting point for dogmatic amplification than the straight lines, the existential standpoint of proclamation. The pattern of dogmatic amplification (kerygmatically no less relevant) we find given in Question 2.

### 3. The Text of the Second Question and Answer

Question 2 speaks of the three points which must be known if we are to actualize in our lives this sole comfort and trust, and which in what follows we recognize to be the three parts of the Catechism. They are: 1. Sin and wretchedness. 2. Redemption. 3. Gratitude.

The very formulation—that these points must be known if I am to live and die happily in this trust—confronts us here with a problem. What kind of knowledge is in question here? Is it a question of the quasi-dogmatic knowledge which is developed in the three parts of the catechism that follow? Is it then being suggested that it is essential to know the 129 questions and answers or to have some equivalent knowledge? This seems in fact to be the meaning of Question 2. For the Catechism is meant for the instruction of Christian people, youth in particular, it is not intended merely for theologians. And Karl Barth writes assuredly with justice about Question 2:

> Powerful and mysterious as is the one trust, it is not something irrational. Here there is something which must be recognized and known. And further, it is not something for a few learned

48

theologians, for a few intellectually endowed people, but for every one. In this respect the Heidelberg Catechism is plain. Question 6 states that "man in the first place is created rightly to know his Creator". We have to "learn the word of God" (Qu. 103), faith is a "kind of knowledge, by which I deem to be true what God has revealed to us in His word" (Qu. 21): to hallow the name of God means in the first place "rightly to know oneself" (Qu. 122). Life in this comfort and trust is then according to this Catechism—and one might add, according to Rom. 12:1—a logical *latreia*, a "reasonable service", as assuredly as the comfort of the gospel is the comfort granted by God Himself. Where God is in question, there also wisdom is in question, and so, for man, recognition and knowledge. This comfort concerns the whole man and hence also the mind and insight of man (*Christliche Lehre* ... pp. 28ff.).

This point of view is in itself doubtless right: the Word of God, the revelation, the trust, is not something irrational (it is a question in fact what this latter word means: it could arise only within the horizons of a rationalistic world-view). It is on the contrary intelligible, understandable and thus far "rational". The question is only: of what character is the understanding, assimilation, knowledge that are demanded?

Question 2 states that knowledge of this kind is necessary in order that man may live and die in comfort and trust. What the Catechism subsequently gives to be known, however, is a far-reaching theological development. And at this point we must criticize the Catechism's failure to understand its own essential character. For the knowledge of the numerous points of the theological explanation (which of course in their straightforward style are comprehensible to non-theologians) cannot be the pre-requisite for living and dying in the one Christian faith. Here we must object to the too rationalistic conception of faith which is inherent in the Catechism. In any case, living and dying in the one true faith, or in other words, faith itself as tested in life and death, is an absolutely existential datum which cannot possibly depend on the knowledge of certain formulae. The "knowledge" demanded by Question 2, if it is really to be an integral part of this existential datum and is really to be necessary for living and dying in the one true faith, must then be a knowledge of a special kind. It is a knowledge, an assimilation, an understanding, that has itself existential character. This knowledge is not only a pre-requisite for faith, for life in trust, but it belongs inalienably to faith.

Hence with regard to the three points of Question 2 which "it is necessary to know" we are basically confronted by structural phases in the whole life of faith. Faith is in fact this knowledge, this appropriation, this understanding. It is in this sense that faith has the character of knowledge. It is by its very nature a kind of knowledge. It implies understanding.[1] Thus "the three points which must be known . . ." are structural elements of existential understanding, which is faith itself. The believer as such grasps just these three things: he realizes that his situation is one of lostness in the eyes of God (sin and wretchedness); he understands the action which God has taken, and experiences an emancipating encounter with God in this situation ("how I . . . am redeemed"); he appreciates finally his engagement resulting from this situation which God has orientated (gratitude).

It must be emphatically pointed out that these three "points" are not three different things, which can be appreciated independently of each other, but rather three necessary and integral parts of the one faith and that they always cohere with and belong to each other. Thus in order to appreciate God's liberating action one must at the same time appreciate the condition of lostness which is thereby overcome and the obligation which arises from it. In order to

---

[1] There is of course an aspect of faith in its living reality, which transcends even this existential understanding and knowledge. It is the "peace which passes all understanding", that gift of God, that divine reality adapted to the measure of man's being, which goes beyond understanding. We have to reckon with this dimension when we speak of faith. Faith as knowledge and understanding remains implicit in and related to this supreme sense of the reality of God. Its relation to the latter is dialectical, and the dialectic may be regarded as immanent within the structure of faith according as to whether we consider the "peace which passes all understanding" as an integral element in faith or not. This point belongs to the problems of pistiology.

realize the lostness of man's condition, his sin and his misery, one would have to grasp already the fact of divine redemption. (This point Karl Barth was constantly stressing, explaining that one understands sin only through the experience of the forgiveness of sins, and that one understands judgment only through the experience of divine grace.) And again one can only appreciate the full seriousness of the command "to live henceforth to Him", when the two other points have been understood.

This seems clear and corresponds truly to what we have already said about the oneness of God, of the faith, of proclamation and of dogmatics. Nevertheless there here intrudes itself on our notice a remarkable situation: we have earlier said that the pure unity of the faith is seldom realized in practice in the psychological realities of human existence, that it rather seems to be always transcended by and grounded only in the unity of God Himself. The inalienable unity with which we are concerned is something we do not meet with empirically. And yet our thought about faith can never cease to presuppose it, since otherwise all we say about faith would necessarily be inappropriate and unreasonable. Theology always understands the discursive movement of its thought only as an analysis of this presupposed unity. Now however it seems that there exists alongside this intellectual analysis of the one and the whole into its structural phases something like a factual, existential, fateful, splitting up of the same. Intrinsically it would seem impossible, for example, to understand judgment apart from grace, or grace apart from judgment. Nevertheless there are found in reality various types of piety, various vocations, various ways in which men walk before God, and it may well happen that a man in his path of life experiences judgment—apparently in dissociation from all else—or grace, again apparently in dissociation from all else (or the challenge to engagement or any other moment in the one saving faith).

It may occur that in one human destiny this or that aspect of the one total faith is seen in an exemplary and isolated fashion, that therefore in fact fate, or life itself, the destiny that God sends, effects the analysis of truth and that it is given to man to bear witness to the one truth of God in this or that particular way. In this matter however (if we assume the truth and reality of God) it is a question of the splitting up of the unity and not of an incoherent plurality. The one truth remains over all, not as a subsequently thought-out synthesis, but as an original unity, which is expressed in the manifold destinies of men in manifold ways. One and the same divine light is broken up and refracted in a multiplicity of colours. But the same thing takes place in preaching, which is carried out "from faith to faith", arising from the manifold ways of men at grips with their divine destiny, and addressing itself again to these multifarious circumstances: whether it be that we proclaim judgment or grace, the cross or the resurrection, or whatever aspect of the divine action with one-sided emphasis and rigour, yet it is always (assuming we succeed in finding the essential word that strikes home) the one Christ that is proclaimed and the one healing and total gospel that is preached. Preaching, because it reflects faith as lived and is rooted in and aims at the actual experience of faith similarly splits up in practice the ultimate unity of the faith.

Despite this existential "spectral analysis of truth" which is analogous and parallel to the theological analysis, the presupposition of original unity remains valid. We have shown that the three points of Question 2 are not only elements placed alongside each other, but cohere with each other, necessarily and inseparably, as structural moments in the one truth. We have further shown that the knowledge of these three points is no book knowledge of principles, but rather that knowledge or understanding which constitutes the very life of faith.

4. *Question 2 as showing the Formal Structure of Kerygmatic and Dogmatic Explanation.*

Understood thus, Question 2 like Question 1 throws light on the analogy and so on the continuity between dogmatics and preaching. Question 1 designated the one object of both, which is thematic in the two spheres in a characteristically different way. It contains in a nutshell the *fides quae creditur*. Question 2, as we have seen, discloses the structural elements of the *fides qua creditur*. In virtue of the inseparability of the *fides quae* and the *fides qua* the structural elements of the latter supply the formal structure for the explication of the former. In other words, the essential structure of faith has to be the guide to the method by which the "matter" of faith is unfolded and explained. This is shown in the Heidelberg Catechism which, after the pattern of the principle designated in Question 2, presents in three parts the matter which is described in Question 1.

This principle of explication is true of both dogmatics and preaching. The latter, in so far as it is genuine, contains implicitly and without question the formal principle of the three points, effective in action. Implicitly, because preaching is direct, in a certain way unreflective and undiscursive, it says quite simply what it has to say. In dogmatics we become reflectively aware of what we already implicitly knew through preaching, and of course in such a way that conscious reflection serves the purpose of future preaching.

Let us look first at preaching. It is carried out according to the pattern of the "three points". First it shows man his sin and wretchedness; it arouses in him a sense of his true situation in the sight of God; it shows him convincingly how he is in truth placed, his predicament; it addresses him on the basis of the factual situation in which he is involved. Secondly, it speaks to him of what God has done, in such a way as to meet the need of his sin and misery; it shows him how God confronts him precisely in the actual situation of his life. Thirdly, it shows him how in this situation and because of his saving encounter with God he is obliged to live for God and to adopt a certain manner of life.

As a rule the individual sermon has these three parts, in this or that order, perhaps interpenetrating each other. Naturally the emphases may be differently distributed in different sermons, according to the text chosen and the pastoral circumstances; they may be placed sometimes on this, sometimes on that one of the "three points"; the parts of the sermon may differ in length. But in principle the sermon as a whole has just these three things to say. Its centre lies in the middle point, in the proclamation of God's action. But in order to be intelligible and effective, this proclamation needs the other two parts, the disclosure of the true situation and the emphasis on the resulting obligation.

Each of the three points poses its own problems homiletically: the disclosure of the true situation must in fact carry conviction and not seem a mere assertion. The challenge to engagement must again strike home and not seem a mere illusory, because unfulfillable, demand. And for the intelligibility of the central part, the proclamation, all depends on its being brought into closest connexion with the two other parts.

As far as dogmatics is concerned, it need not necessarily be arranged in three parts according to the pattern of the Heidelberg Catechism. Other arrangements are certainly conceivable. Nevertheless dogmatics must consistently observe in all its developments the pattern of the "three points". For in all its passages dogmatics has an eye on preaching. Like preaching it again is concerned to declare God's mighty action. In so doing it constantly bears in mind the actual situation of man and his obligation. Thus the analysis of the human predicament and the study of ethical obligation should not really exist as independent disciplines alongside dogmatics but should rather penetrate and inform dogmatics. This is manifestly the case in the work of Karl Barth, who in his *Church Dogmatics* inserts his ethical developments (ethics of creation and ethics of divine providence) in various contexts. Every essentially dogmatic passage should, *eo ipso*, just because it is dogmatic, contain implications for the actual situation of man and his ethical obligations. Dogmatics is concerned with the intimate connexion between these different aspects—and in this lies the reason for the difference between its method of explication and that characteristic of preaching, for the latter does not think out and show this connexion with scientific rigour, but rather, in virtue of its immediate intuition of the pastoral circumstances and the bearing of the text, reveals it directly as a living force.

Finally as regards dogmatics we must note that, despite our criticism of the Heidelberg Catechism which led us to understand the "knowledge" of Question 2 not as dogmatic knowledge of doctrine but as the existential knowledge proper to faith itself, nevertheless dogmatic developments do arise out of the latter by way of explication. The continuity between dogmatic treatment and the original existential knowledge remains unimpaired.

### Theses developed in Chapter 2.

5. Dogmatics and preaching resemble each other and cohere with each other in the fact that they unfold and amplify one and the same truth. Both are characterized by the same structural explication of an original unity. Hence neither of them has to do with a plurality of things to be believed or with "saving facts", but with one sole reality, with the one God and Lord and with faith in this Lord.

6. An essential difference between dogmatics and preaching lies in the mode in which they unfold and explain the one truth given to them both. Dogmatics is adapted to take a systematic and synoptic view. Preaching on the other hand unfolds the total truth of the gospel *ad hoc*, from one angle, having regard to the special characteristics of the text and the pastoral situation.

7. The Heidelberg Catechism designates in Question 1 the "one comfort and trust" which forms the presupposition and ground of both dogmatics and preaching. The heart of this description and the real kerygma lies in the statement that man is not his own master, but that he is surrendered to Another, the Lord. This brings forward to our notice an elemental situation with its challenge, which in its simplicity cannot be further explained, but which is understandable as a summons. Further, Question 1 contains characteristically as the first amplification of this central truth the dogmatic motives of the cross, divine providence, eternal life and the Christian way of life.

8. For the understanding of this central kerygmatic statement it is essential to realize that not only is man delivered from his self-dominion but is confronted by the Lord Himself as the supreme Disposer.

9. Faith as implying life in this "sole trust" is by its very nature an existential knowledge and understanding. The latter has three necessarily inseparable structural phases; the believer's realization of his own situation as one of lostness, his realization of the liberating act of God, and of the obligation for man which arises from it (Qu. 2).

10. This inner structure of faith yields the principle governing the explication of the one truth which is the ground of both

preaching and dogmatics. Preaching has necessarily these three moments: disclosure of the human predicament, proclamation of the act of God, and appeal to walk in newness of life. Similarly dogmatic explication must point in these three directions, though the plan of dogmatics need not necessarily follow for that reason the threefold pattern of the Heidelberg Catechism.

# PART TWO

## CLARIFICATION OF THE PRO-GRAMME IN THE LIGHT OF THE DOCTRINE OF SIN

The first and the shortest of the three parts of the Heidelberg Catechism contains the reference to the situation of mankind. Man's situation in the sight of God is one of wretchedness. This wretchedness has its root in sin. If we wish to use more "modern" words, then we may say: man without God is homeless. His homelessness, that is, his state of being without God, is rooted in his guilt. The latter becomes actual in view of the divine law which can be summed up in the twofold law of love. This, however, man cannot keep, has not in fact kept, and does not keep (Qu. 3 to 5).

In what follows (Qu. 6 to 9) objections are set aside, objections which attempt to explain this harsh situation on speculative lines and so try to soften it. At the same time, by the refutation of these objections, the situation—such as it is—is further elucidated. Finally (in Qu. 10 and 11) the seriousness of the universal situation as regards guilt is still further emphasized by the introduction of the ideas of the wrath and righteousness of God. It is shown as a radical disturbance of man's relation with God, and thus the disclosure of man's predicament in the eyes of God is completed. Thus ends the sweep of this first main part.

We shall now follow this curve and consider the particular questions from the general point of view of a "disclosure of the situation", which we have learnt to recognize as one of the three decisive moments of preaching. Basically it is here a question of the right proclamation of sin and judgment, of the clarifying dogmatic categories which must be borne in mind when preaching on this theme. In this connexion we

57

shall have to speak first of the concept of law and of the position and function of the kerygma of judgment within the kerygma as a whole. Secondly we shall have to consider the concrete manifestation of law in the twofold law of love, after which, thirdly, the problem of original sin and the fall will present itself to us. We shall deepen and render more precise the insight into guilt (which is in question here) by, fourthly, concerning ourselves with the radical nature of sin and the slavery of the will. Fifthly and finally we must give consideration to the concept of the wrath of God.

Such are the dogmatic motives which in their interconnexion form the basis of the first main part and in which sin and judgment—a theme of preaching—are clarified in conscious reflection.

# CHAPTER 3

# THE LAW OF GOD AS A POINT OF DEPARTURE

(Heidelberg Catechism, Question 3.)

Question 3. **"From what source do you come to understand your misery? From the law of God."**

### 1. *Law and Historical Man*

THE GENERAL problem of our discussion springs from the proclamation of sin and judgment. Preaching must always develop the theme of man's sin and the misery which flows from it, man's guilt and homelessness. This theme is not simply a part but belongs integrally to the whole proclamation of the Kyrios, the kerygma, of Him to whom as my true keeper I am surrendered, such surrender constituting my sole comfort in life and death. Christian preaching is therefore—just because in all its manifestations it is a development of this one central kergyma—always inclusive of the preaching of sin and judgment. I mean that it is so even when it does not speak explicitly of sin and judgment. But again and again this essential and always implicit moment must become manifest, it must also be proclaimed explicitly. Thus this theme requires special dogmatic clarification.

In the first place it may here be explained, from a terminological point of view, that in using the concepts of sin and misery, homelessness and guilt, we are denoting the very thing which it is customary to describe, in the categories of modern existentialist philosophy, as an existence in decadence or unreality—expressions which have won a place in this circle of ideas with Bultmann and his school. Man's being in sin and misery is perhaps more strikingly expressed and seized upon by the use of such existential concepts and terms. For the old ideas are today in danger of being moralistically understood and so misunderstood. A moralistic proclamation of sin and judgment (at least today) has ceased to have any effect on the hearer. The preacher must mark this! For the traditional theological and edificatory talk of sin and judgment has moralistic overtones. Whoever preaches unoriginally, which means disingenuously and thoughtlessly, superficially adopts such clichés and so misses the mark.

It may very well be true that for an earlier epoch the moralistic pattern of thought supplied a genuine symbol of what is truly meant and that therefore the truth was understood. But even so, only a symbol! For in any event far more is in question than what society calls morals. Today one can no longer reckon with a moral consciousness generally accepted as valid. Hence there is no point in preaching with moral reproaches. The fact of sin must be preached otherwise, and in its essence it is more than merely moral failing. In this connexion the use of existentialist philosophical categories, or, more correctly, the language of existence itself, may denote a real step forward in the recognition of the essential truth, and any such language may therefore be a real help homiletically. These concepts show the preacher, better than any moralistic scheme, what is really at stake in the doctrine of man's sin and misery, and thus enable him to attain a more exact and appropriate style of preaching.

There is no need for me to explain in detail here these existential concepts of reality or unreality (decadence) which essentially, in the truths they express, go back to Kierkegaard. In any case they are intended to convey the line of thought as to whether man is "himself" or not, whether he "exists" in the truth or not. Existence in unreality at once implies sin and misery, guilt and homelessness, and contains implicitly the idea of judgment. The judgment which overshadows the man who exists without God consists in his very existence without God. That is man's misery! Insights of this kind are to be found in the Old Testament. Take for instance the 73rd Psalm and the masterly interpretation of it given by Buber (in *Recht und Unrecht*, Basle, 1952[1])—an interpretation which he himself describes as existential. (For example vv. 18 to 20 which, Buber thinks, refer to ultimate nothingness, to the sheer unreality of the outwardly perhaps happy and prosperous existence of the godless: "Truly Thou dost set them in slippery places, thou dost make them fall to ruin, How they are destroyed in a moment, swept away utterly by terrors! They are like a dream when one awakes, on awaking you

[1] E.T. *Right and Wrong*, 1952.

despise their phantoms.'') So much for terminological clarification. It can be seen that modern existential terms are better understood today, but furthermore and above all they contribute to a better understanding of the thing itself.

Whenever it has to speak of man's misery, the Heidelberg Catechism immediately recurs to the idea of law. The idea of the law is thus the vehicle by which the human situation of unreality is made apparent. No doubt there is much in favour of the thesis of Bultmann, Gerhard Ebeling and others who simply equate the law with the concrete historical realities of human life, or at least bring it into closest connexion with this. Man under the law is historical man, man in his actual historical situations and responsibilities. Hence man in his responsibility before God and his existence under the judgment of God; man in his essential and inescapable confrontation by God; to put it briefly, man in the historical dimension of his life. Whether he wills it or not, whether he realizes it or not, man lives his life in the sight of God. Whether he likes it or not, man is a historical being.

The "medium" of such living in the sight of God, of such historical creatureliness, in fact the medium of all Godward relationship, is called the law. Hence preaching can address man in no other way than as a historical being, that is, as man under the law. In this view the law is not a special aspect or theme of proclamation, but its entire all-embracing horizon. Proclamation moves within the horizons and through the medium of the law. It goes without saying that here the concept of the law has been extended far beyond the concept of law in the Old Testament. (In this circle of ideas Rom. 2:14 would belong, the passage about the heathen who nevertheless have the law of God "written in their hearts"—assuming that the traditional interpretation of the verse is correct.) Further it seems to us that from the standpoint of this conception of the law, gospel and law can no longer be regarded quite simply as polar opposites (as they are regarded in current theology) and that we must rather accept the idea of a kind of interpenetration, or interchangeability of law and gospel. None the less it remains true to say that according to this broadest understanding of the law, the law is the presupposition for the event of the gospel. But may such a presupposition be understood as a preparatory stage? It is in fact extremely questionable how far the law, apart from the gospel, could be recognized by us. Would it not be a recognition of God apart from Jesus Christ, which means however an encounter with God that is not from the start qualified by the fact of the divine incarnation in Jesus Christ?

## 2. *Law and Gospel*

We ask first about the meaning and purpose of Question 3 in the total context of our discussion, our problem concerning the disclosure of the human predicament through preaching and dogmatics. Where is the point of departure, where the criterion for such a disclosure? Even in the law of God. Thus we are referred back to God: the sequence of thought has, as it were, been bent backwards to God. We have no other basis for the recognition of man's guilt and homelessness in the eyes of God but that of God Himself. This means that the understanding of human sin and misery is not a purely profane human self-understanding and self-criticism hovering in the void, arising prior to and apart from any encounter with God.

This insight of course implies human self-knowledge and human self-criticism, but from its very inception it is aroused by the atmosphere, the inspiration of the law, which is no human law, but the law *of God*. (Cf. on this point the thought, which was so decisive for Calvin, of the continuity between knowledge of God and knowledge of the self, *Inst.* 1559, I, 1, 2.) With the self-knowledge flowing from the disclosure of human misery, we move from the start within the "circle of knowledge of God". We are moving in the circle which is described by Question 1, for of course the dogmatic programme which aims at the unfolding of the one truth requires a circular movement of thought, since the thinker, proceeding from the one and unfolding it, remains necessarily within its sphere and influence. The God whose law enables us to know the depth of our misery is none other than the "Lord", our true sovereign and master, named in Question 1. Hence the knowledge of the law of God and the understanding of human misery which flows from it cannot be as it were an independent preparatory stage, an outer court, from which man could climb to the sanctuary of the knowledge of the gospel. For this reason the current idea of a gradation from law to grace, or law to gospel, is to be rejected.

Thus by a second line of thought, namely the consideration of the continuity between Question 3 and Question 1, we have reached the same goal as previously through our examination of the broad conception of the law. Here there emerges a new dogmatic conception of the law by which preaching must be orientated. Perhaps however this specific understanding of the law springs likewise from homiletic, kerygmatic motives. We must at this point ask the question whether the type of preaching which proceeds from law to grace or from law to the gospel is right and effective? At times this has been in fact the type of sermon advocated: man should first be shattered by the proclamation of the law, convicted in his conscience and exposed as a lost sinner so that afterwards the proferred grace in Christ could most effectively be declared to him. And no doubt many a sermon has been preached on these lines. But is this doctrine, this dualistic understanding of the relation between law and gospel, the right one and is the preaching based on it honest preaching?

Before going into this question, we would at this point observe that Karl Barth in his commentary on the Heidelberg Catechism decidedly rejects the gradation from law to gospel, which is of course first and foremost of homiletic relevance. Such a repudiation, he thinks, is suggested by the mere outward form and arrangement of the Catechism:

First, it is in general quite striking how much shorter is this first part than the two which follow. This is not without its significance. . . . What we hear in Questions 3 to 9 and 10 to 11, is, as we have already noted, included in the idea of comfort and trust. It is not drawn from some alien source, but from the one Christian truth, and hence it may not be developed in abstraction. . . . What is here in question is the initial situation of the man who has to do with Jesus Christ. It is not the unbeliever who will truly recognize this initial situation, not man before his regeneration, but the man who has already hearkened to the glad tidings of the gospel of grace. He it is who understands human misery. The emphatic negatives pronounced against humanity in its misery, as expressed in Questions 5, 6, and 9, are only possible from that ultimate standpoint from which again they cannot be a final word. For from the standpoint of the gospel man is never seen in himself but ever only as the soul who is in the keeping of his true Saviour.

Finally:

It is just those who know the word of God, who are ready and willing to hear it, and who cling to the one comfort in life and in death, who know also that they are such as break God's law. (pp. 30ff.).

Clearly Barth here argues, without saying so himself, precisely on the lines of that dogmatic scheme which requires that all dogmatic developments must be an unfolding of the one truth (in fact the whole of Barth's theology, without being fully conscious of this, proceeds on these lines; it is a theology which in all its parts must be understood from this point of view, or else it is so easily misunderstood!). Judgment is only to be understood as "included in the one comfort and trust". The recognition of it is "drawn from the one Christian truth and hence it may not be developed in abstraction". Such recognition must rather be developed as a moment in the one truth, the one faith. And it is not unregenerate man, but precisely man as believer in Jesus Christ and the gospel of grace, who also through his belief understands divine judgment. In other words, there cannot be in principle any recognition of and belief in divine judgment apart from faith in the grace which has been manifested in Jesus Christ.

Thus in consequence of applying the principle of an unfolding of the one truth, instead of the current dualism of law and gospel, we find that we have to do with a "monism", which suggests that the one and sole comfort implies both things, judgment and grace, law and gospel. The law of God is the presupposition for the understanding of the gospel and is inherent in the gospel, but it is not a preparatory stage which must needs be gone through and left behind. In the gospel God is recognized as the God of law, and the gospel in itself upholds the law: the responsibility of men before God, and the basic requirement of God, in fact, everything for which the term "law" is an inclusive concept, remains valid after as before Christ. The *sola gratia* and the *sola fide* "apart from the works of the law" are in no wise impaired in consequence! For the sole efficacious reality of grace belongs to the very idea of the gospel, to the very essence of the one faith and trust, and in Question I, which yields the one truth to be unfolded, it is for sure implicitly contained. It remains the *articulus stantis et cadentis ecclesiae*, by which the Church stands or falls; for without the *sola gratia*, without the *sola fide*, God would not be God! The current dualistic scheme with its corresponding homiletics and dogmatics is by no means indispensable for the understanding and proclamation of this truth. In order to understand the *sola gratia* one does not need to construct any preparatory stage of mere knowledge of the law.

We have in this argument shaken an inveterate, deeply rooted theological position and we owe a few words in justification: as a dogmatic argument we claim that, on the presupposition of the principle that dogma is an unfolding of the one truth, no other position is tenable for us. But to this there corresponds a kerygmatic argument. Barth's insight into the fact that judgment is implicitly contained in the one trust, hence the cancellation of the dualism between law and gospel, can and must be homiletically based as well. Thus we come back to the question posed earlier about the practical "existential" rightness and effectiveness of a sermon which is divided into the two stages of law and gospel. It seems to us that this type of sermon is in the last resort disingenuous and therefore ineffective. This of course does not preclude the possibility of constructing some particular sermon, on occasion, after this pattern. But such a scheme must not become a necessarily postulated rule. For the dishonesty would consist in this, that the initiated would realize from the outset that judgment would be followed by grace, the crushing law by the uplifting gospel. In this way, the law, and—in so far as the latter is a precondition for the experience of the gospel—the gospel itself, would no longer be taken really seriously.

No doubt it is true to say that to the proclamation of grace belongs also that of judgment, to the proclamation of the gospel belongs also necessarily that of the law. The situation of wretchedness must be so depicted that grace is understood and taken seriously. But such a description cannot be allowed to become an independent prior condition. Rather is it from the start relative to the kerygma of grace and is implicit in the latter. Just inasmuch as I proclaim the God of mercy, I proclaim also the God of judgment. Not otherwise! Thus far may the gospel be said to be the condition for the understanding of the law. He who has not understood the meaning of grace, how should he understand the meaning of sin and judgment? Such a one has not yet encountered the living God!

As we have said, we cannot today reckon with an unimpaired, generally accepted system of morals or of natural law. An autonomous doctrine of pervasive universal justice and of retribution and recompense, a preaching of future punishment in hell would be of no use. For in a time of nihilism and the dissolution of values it simply would not be believed. And this is perhaps just as well. Only when we proclaim the gospel of the grace of God in Jesus Christ, only when we present God Himself in our sermon as the living God of grace, can the message of the law, of sin and of judgment become convincing. Only so will the hearer understand that being without God is plainly being in utter nothingness. In our day there is hardly a greater hindrance to the understanding of judgment and therewith of grace than the current moralistic talk about "sin" and the "sinner". I repeat and emphasize that all this is true of our own time and that in other times the situation may have been different. The moral standards of an epoch are a phenomenon which belongs to the history of the human spirit. These subordinate conditions for the understanding and reception of the gospel may change in the course of history.

In catechism classes we may well on occasion make use of the scheme which sees law and gospel as stages, for from a purely didactic point of view it helps us to clarify a situation, namely the situation in which law and gospel belong together. In catechesis, in church instruction, it is a question primarily of mental drill in certain concepts characteristic of scripture and doctrine, undertaken merely as a preparation for the understanding of the Word as preached. In preaching, however, where what is at issue is something ultimate, a life-and-death matter, "conversion", we must, out of sheer honesty, renounce the use of a formal pattern. Let it still make its appearance occasionally at times when the sermon assumes a didactic and catechetical character. Yet not without being immediately relativized. Thus in preaching it is not a question of two acts, judgment and grace, but of one single act, namely, grace which implies judgment. Just so will the full seriousness of both judgment and grace be appreciated. But in this respect dogmatics, because its concern is with the truth itself and not with any preparatory "drill", has little in common with homiletics and catechesis!

Thus we hope to have rendered convincing, both from a dogmatic and from a homiletic point of view, Karl Barth's thesis about the relation of law and gospel, so clearly exemplified in the Heidelberg Catechism. Moreover here we have a new illustration of the continuity and reciprocal effects of proclamation and dogmatics.

This thesis of Barth is reflected again in what he says concerning the criterion for the realization of human wretchedness:

Here it is not simply a question of a human indictment, the expressions found in Questions 3 to 9 have not arisen from either optimism or pessimism, they arise rather from the hearing of the law of God. . . . And in this confrontation the decision is made: man is wicked. . . . "None is righteous, no, not one" (Rom. 3:10). "Every imagination of the thoughts of his heart is only evil continually" (Gen. 6:5). Such then is man, but the picture results not from some power of self-judgment, but rather from what God has spoken to him (pp. 33ff.).

No objection can be made to this point of view. It is God's judgment, not our own power of self-criticism, which convinces us of our sin and misery. None the less Barth could at this point be misunderstood and has in fact in some quarters been misunderstood. It is not of course sufficient for the preacher to greet his hearers with the abstract assertion: In the judgment of God you are a lost sinner! Rather a concrete picture must be drawn showing convincingly the guilt and homelessness in the life of the hearer. The assertion must be made evident to the hearer, it must be brought home to him in concrete illustration, that he may accept it. This however must be done by "confrontation", that is, without the sermon deteriorating into a simple amplification of human self-judgments on the basis of moral, sociological, psycho-analytic criteria and such like. The picture must be drawn concretely, with reference to the daily life of men just as it is, and yet precisely there, in constant confrontation with the living and gracious God without whom the life of man, of whatever kind it be, is sheer nothingness. In this true concrete delineation of the ultimate situation, implying law, sin, and judgment, lies one of the greatest difficulties of Christian preaching. The preacher must overcome it in absolute honesty, with serious observation of the true deep situation in himself and in others, and with utter responsibility and concern.

### Theses developed in Chapter 3

11. Christian preaching is always implicitly a reflection of the whole of Christian truth and therefore also becomes from time to time an explicit proclamation of sin and judgment. It addresses man with respect to his innermost and real situation in which he finds himself to be lost in the sight of God. Thus it speaks of

what modern existential thought, unmoralistic and therefore the more appropriate, denotes by the existential phrase "unreality of existence". In such a phrase are summed up the realities of sin and judgment.

12. In Question 3 of the Heidelberg Catechism the concept of the divine law is the vehicle by which is conveyed such a disclosure of the real human situation in the sight of God. The term "law" signifies in this connexion the concrete historical reality of human existence as an existence lived in the sight of God, as a "walking before the face of God", and so under God's demand. Thus law is both the horizon and the medium of every earthly human life lived in relation with God.

13. The gospel is not to be proclaimed apart from the law, nor the law apart from the gospel. The type of preaching which arranges law and gospel in stages, which makes the pure preaching of the law an independent and necessary preparatory stage to the preaching of the gospel, is to be rejected as kerygmatically disingenuous and dogmatically incorrect (because it does not fulfil the dogmatic idea of the unfolding of the one truth). Law and gospel, judgment and grace are to be proclaimed as one single theme.

CHAPTER 4

# GOD'S DEMAND AND MAN'S FAILURE
(The concrete actualization of the divine law.)
(Heidelberg Catechism, Questions 4 and 5.)

Question 4. **"What then does the divine law require of us?
Christ teaches us this in a summary of the law given in Matt.
22.: 'You shall love the Lord your God with all your heart
and with all your soul, and with all your mind. This is the
great and first commandment. And a second is like it. You
shall love your neighbour as yourself. On these two commandments depend all the law and the prophets.'"** Question 5.
**"Can you keep this law perfectly? No, for I am by nature
inclined to hate God and my neighbour."**

## 1. *The Unity of the Command*

THE LAW is the all-embracing horizon of Christian
proclamation. Man lives his whole life within the sphere
of the law. He walks before the face of God. The law
challenges man and decrees his responsibility. What the law
requires of us and to what extent we fulfil its requirements,
we learn from Questions 3 and 4 of the Catechism. Here the
law and the human situation which is based on it assume
concrete form. It is conceivable that at this point we might
expatiate on the decalogue. For the ten commandments are
certainly the "ordinances of the covenant of grace", they
are "ordinances meant to govern the lives of those to whom
God has manifested His love and grace" (Barth). Thus they
might well be considered to prescribe the area within which
man stands responsible before God, to indicate the horizon
within which he "walks before God's countenance". None
the less the authors of the Heidelberg Catechism have
reserved the treatment of the ten commandments for the
third main part. There, under the title "Of man's thankfulness", the commandments appear from the point of view of

70

the *tertius usus legis*, hence from the point of view of sanctification. Nevertheless here too in the first main part, so soon as the sequence of thought strikes the divine law, the latter must be expressed concretely. This takes place through the summary of the two laws, the twofold law of love.

The concrete expression of the law which we find in Question 4 has its specific dogmatic and homiletic meaning. It suggests something which is essential for Christian proclamation: primarily *the unity of the law*. The law of God—in this respect unlike codifications of human law—is not a codex with many specific commands, but one single requirement, corresponding to the unity of the one God. Even the ten commandments are at bottom merely manifestations of this one single requirement; and even the twofold law of love constitutes in its dual aspect one single law.[1] ("The second is like it. . . ." This does not mean of like dignity, but is meant to convey that in the second part of the command it is a question of one and the same requirement—and in this interpretation of ours we claim to be establishing not "historical" but essential truth!)

From this there follows, with respect to the understanding of sin, something of equal importance for Christian proclamation: namely, that man is not a sinner because he transgresses the various statutes of a codex, for example a moral codex, but because he fails to fulfil the one essential requirement addressed to his being as man. And lastly, and in consequence, it follows that judgment on sin is not to be understood as a punishment for transgressions, but it exists rather because man has not the capacity to fulfil the one requirement. It is in this way that both sin and judgment upon sin are to be preached; and again, it is such a preaching about sin that will be understood in our time.

And this is not because it is suitable to the needs of "modern man", but because, perhaps under the compulsion of the modern age and its problems, it best fits the Word

[1] Cf. Luther's interpretation of the commandments in the Short Catechism, with its constantly recurring opening: "We are to fear and love God, in order that. . . ."

of God, because it proclaims God Himself and nothing else, not some moral or religious system of thought. The living God Himself is essentially the one basic demand overshadowing man's being, and the absence of God from man's life is in itself the judgment. (The formulation that God Himself is His one requirement would of course need a closer interpretation!)

Now the unity of the divine law which has thus disclosed itself to us is no abstract unity, but rather, just because it is the unity of God Himself, it is a concrete reality to be unfolded, explicated and applied *in concreto*, on the lines suggested by our dogmatic theme. God Himself is no divine abstraction, hovering over all, pervasive in all, but because He is the omnipresent One, He is the God of every human life, the sovereign Lord present in a specific manner in each individual life, and just so is He the ever living God, the supreme concrete reality. Thus the unity of His one essential command will be thoroughly actualized, made concrete, in the individual commands, in the "commands for the hour", always according to the situation in which man is confronted by God. This concrete translation of the one essential command into a "command for the hour", as also the concrete translation of the message concerning the divine judgment on sin (for judgment also, the absence of God, can be manifested to men in the most varied ways) will be effected in preaching. For this reason preaching is essentially related to a given situation.

Dogmatics is related to situation in so far as it always keeps in mind the possibility of concrete situations. Preaching however has always to do with concrete situations. A sermon which is totally unrelated to any concrete situation is simply not possible. Since however Sunday by Sunday we cannot have in view an actual pastoral situation common to all the members of the congregation, we need something to help us, in order that we may nevertheless pierce to the heart of some concrete situation. Such a help is to be found in the text of the sermon. The text, itself born out of a living situation, and still after centuries redolent of the circumstances which gave rise to it, places in our hand some situation (or numerous related situations) which might well

72

resemble the particular circumstances in which some members of our congregation find themselves placed. The text of our sermon therefore, as it were, takes the place of an unequivocally clear common pastoral situation which is lacking. Moreover because it is a text from the past and from Holy Scripture it contains much more than the suggestion of a concrete situation: it contains the living gospel operative in such a situation. Of course the actual or potential situation in which an individual member of the congregation is placed also contains the promise of the gospel, in so far as each individual man is in fact ever confronted by the living God, by Jesus Christ. But it contains the gospel only as a promise, latently. The Gospel has not yet brought such a situation to a final issue. For our human eyes it is difficult or impossible to recognize the gospel in such situations. Hence as a rule we need the guidance of a Biblical text. For the essence of a Biblical text is this: that it springs from the heart of a situation in which the gospel has already brought matters to a final issue.

Thus the concrete expression of the law in Question 4 gives pointers for the concrete disclosure of situation in the act of preaching. Dogmatics finds here a formulation which becomes an obligatory norm for preaching. Dogmatics is concerned to reach the truth (in this case the truth of the divine law); it attempts to know the truth and to formulate it, but it does so (and this could well be the specific characteristic of dogmatic knowledge of the truth as distinct from every other kind of knowledge) in the constant realization— a realization which shapes the whole course of its thinking —that here it is a question of a truth which can only spring to light and be actualized in the word of the preacher, in a living challenge to man, in the concrete act of church proclamation. Dogmatic thinking and dogmatic formulations must ever be stamped by the realization of the specific character of the truth which dogma seeks. One must be able to recognize in such formulations and to show in them the mark of their origin, the fact that they have arisen from this kind of knowledge and consist in it.

Thus the dogmatic insight into the unity of the divine law which we have deduced from the formulation of Question 4 contains an intimation for preaching. We have seen that this insight guides preaching about sin and the divine judgment on sin in a specific direction. This insight into the unity of the divine law absolutely excludes—and for the very reason that it is no abstract unity, but unity of such a kind as may be concretely embodied in, sharpened into a "law for the hour"—every kind of casuistry in the approach to sin and the divine command which the sinner fails utterly to keep. For casuistry never reaches the *concretissimum* of the non-interchangeable, the unique situation which we have characterized by the phrase "command for the hour", because the very essence of all casuistry is to subsume the particular under the more general. This method of subsumption however can never press forward to reach the divine command addressed to the crisis of the moment. Although we may divide up a line into ever smaller parts, we never reach the point. Casuistry, the system of subsumption, is the hallmark of human as opposed to divine jurisprudence and justice. The gospel, just because it is concerned with the one God, excludes casuistical ethics. Our preaching must note this and remain faithful here. That preaching must bring into the light of this ultimate command, this utterly non-casuistical ethic, human systems of law and morals with the casuistry which is essentially inherent in them, is something that goes without saying: for thus preaching remains related to practical life. It must seriously concern itself about the spirit shaping human ordinances, as the Christian too inasmuch as he is also a citizen of the state must feel himself to be in part responsible for them, so that the ultimate and essential command may somehow make itself felt, manifest itself even in human institutions. None the less the two kinds of ethics and law must never be interchanged or allowed to grow mingled and confused.

## 2. *Love as the Sole Content of the Law*

Question 4 however makes the law of God still more concrete and thus provides further intimations for preaching, that is, for the disclosure of the true human situation. It notes that the disclosure of the unreality of human existence is related on the one hand to the relation between man and God, and, on the other, to the relation between man and man. It establishes further that the unreality of human existence consists in the lack of love.

Here one should speak of love as the distinguishing characteristic of real existence. I do not propose to embark on the adventure of such a dogmatic analysis here, but, as a dogmatist, leave the illustration of this concept and theme to the preacher, without however disowning the dogmatic problem which it implies. Here again we see how fluid are the boundaries between dogmatics and preaching! I assign here to preaching what can and must be soon the theme of dogmatics. I leave to the concrete style and delineation of the preacher with his personal challenges something that may certainly become an object of analytic treatment and clarification also. Dogmatics and preaching are not only concerned with the same truth, they have also the same extension: the same actual questions are posed to both. Yet at times they can temporarily assign limits to each other. The dogmatist can, for example, as I have just done, propose to himself: I will take my analysis this time to such and such a point; the rest I leave to the preacher alone; he must say in his situation what I have not yet been able to analyse. Only such a demarcation of boundaries must not be regarded as final. The preacher may need and desire new clarification and enlightenment, in which case the dogmatist must carry his work beyond the boundaries which he has himself imposed.

I may justify my renunciation of any attempt to develop the concept of *agape* by the consideration that the Catechism itself, while using the concept, does not really clarify it. It may strike us however (and especially in view of preaching) that in our context love appears as *something which man has not*. In the fact of lovelessness lies human sin and misery. We should take care not to speak and preach about the Christian love of neighbour too positively, too optimistically, too emotionally. For in the context of the gospel love is precisely that which we have not, that which, in point of fact, is not to be found in us. Hence in the framework of the disclosure of man's true situation and its concrete delineation, the idea of love plays a negative part, as it were. And it is just in this negative function that it serves the purpose of delineation. In such a picture man must be shown as afflicted with lovelessness. This of course presupposes that, even though the required love is scarcely traceable in human life, it is nevertheless understood what love is.

### 3. *Hate Towards God and Neighbour*

In preaching, the concept of love serves to throw into relief what the positive human frame of mind, and hence what the positive determination of existence in unreality, is. This positive disposition of man living in unreality is hate towards God and neighbour, about which Question 5 speaks.

Quite early, this answer was felt to be offensive and obnoxious. Karl Sudhoff in his *Theologisches Handbuch zur Auslegung des Heidelberger Katechismus* (1862) characterizes this attitude of repugnance towards the answer as Pelagian and Arminian. He calls those who think and express themselves thus "sentimental people" and adds that "it is good for youth to be led early to a real realization of man's corruption and thus to be induced to humble themselves before God and to seek the Saviour". "It is unmistakably clear that all opposition to the fifth question has its root in the denial of the whole depth of human sin and misery. For everything here, even the phrasing, is founded on scripture." At this point all those texts might be quoted (they are especially Pauline and Johannine) which speak of the longings of the σάρξ and of the refusal to recognize the Christ whom God has sent, as an ἔχθρα εἰς Θεόν (hostility to God; Rom. 8:7). Sudhoff and the orthodox champions of Question 5 in the Heidelberg Catechism are of course right in maintaining that its assertion of man's radical guilt in the eyes of God should not be toned down, that nothing in the passage should be relativized. However, the feeling of repugnance to Question 5 may have another and a deeper reason. For in truth the listener to sermons is not so easily convinced about his hatred towards God and neighbour. And that not because he is unwilling to humble himself before God, but simply because from a psychological point of view the reproach is not just.

It is not usually possible to show convincingly that a feeling of hatred exists, if the latter is seen as a psychological datum. The preacher must not be so self-willed as to try to demonstrate its existence to his hearers, if he does not wish to run the risk of ceasing to be listened to. The fact is that hatred towards God and neighbour, mentioned in Question 5, should not be understood psychologically. And in truth the New Testament ἔχθρα εἰς Θεόν is not intended to convey the idea of a subjective feeling but of an objective situation. ῎Εχθρα in this sense means more and is more comprehensive than the mere particular psychological datum of an expressed feeling of hatred. Lovelessness as the actual disposition of human existence, the absence of love as the positive orientation of man living in unreality is in fact—objectively considered and without for the most part man's being aware of it—hatred and enmity, ἔχθρα εἰς Θεόν καὶ εἰς τοὺς ἀνθρώπους. The loveless man is God's enemy. And lovelessness can of course be shown to be the dominating reality of human life, especially in regard to the relations between man and his neighbour. Here man can be convicted of his ἔχθρα. It is more difficult in regard to man's relation with God. For what in truth is the real meaning of loving God. In order to be clearly understood, the preacher will do best in this matter to speak about man's self-examination and self-knowledge (his use of his time, his inner honesty, his self-understanding etc.). In such points as these, man's direct relation with God may most easily be understood, on psychological, empirical lines; in such ways, man's attitude towards God is most clearly seen. Thus man can be best brought to realize the basic falseness in his relation to God.

It thus becomes clear how important is the psychological point of view at times in the preacher's task of disclosing the true human predicament. Yet in all this it is not a question of any sort of psychological doctrine, but of a calm and dispassionate observation of psychological realities.

All in all we think that we have thus attained an understanding of Question 5 which does not in the least weaken the radical nature of man's guilt, and which yet does not expect the listener to sermons to entertain notions about himself which have no correspondence with his empirical self-knowledge.

### Theses developed in Chapter 4.

14. Question 4 makes the divine law concrete through the demand to love God and neighbour. Thus man under the law sees himself ultimately confronted not by a multiplicity of prescripts, but by one sole requirement which concerns the whole of conduct, and which is none the less highly concrete in its challenges. By this means any sort of casuistry in the development of a Christian ethic is excluded.

15. The actual situation of man before God is to be defined by his failure in the love that is required of him. To this extent he is incapable of meeting the essential demand made on his life. The "hatred towards God and neighbour", of which Question 5 speaks, designates the "objective" actual situation of man in the face of God, but for the sake of honesty in preaching must not be misunderstood to connote a demonstrable psychological datum.

CHAPTER 5

# THE FALL OF MAN AND ORIGINAL SIN

(Heidelberg Catechism, Questions 6 and 7)

Question 6. **"Did God then create man wicked and perverse? No, God created man good and after His own image, that is, in true righteousness and holiness, so that man might rightly know his creator, and love Him from the heart and live with Him in eternal blessedness, praising Him for evermore."**
Question 7. **"Whence comes then such corruption in man's nature? From the fall and disobedience of our first parents Adam and Eve in paradise, whence our nature was so tainted, that we are all conceived and born in sin."**

1. *Speculative Thinking and Thinking According to the Exigencies of the Situation*

A SPECULATIVE objection to the demonstration of sin is brought forward and rejected (Qu. 6). The speculative character of the objection consists in this, that the one who thus argues is attempting to break free from his actual existential situation before God, from the situation of guilt and the required assumption of guilt, by escaping into the realm of pure thought, the realm of the speculative. Were it true that God had created man "thus wicked and perverse", then man's situation before God would be deprived of its personal character. Responsibility would be suspended. There would no longer be any room for the concept of guilt. All would be fate.

Here again we note the continuity between preaching and dogmatics: the dogmatic train of thought, which we recognize here, the rejection of the idea of fate overshadowing life and excluding guilt, is an intimation that preaching must hold fast to the theme of guilt, responsibility and freedom, that it must seize man in his actual, personal, responsibility and freedom, that it must seize man in his

79

actual, personal, responsible situation before God. Thus preaching is regulated and controlled by the dogmatic sequence of thought, the dogmatic formulation, and vice versa. In this case dogmatics marks out and defines by its doctrinal formulations a truth which in preaching cannot be called in question. In fact, preaching would become impossible, it would surrender the very possibility of its own functioning, were it to yield in the slightest degree at this point, were it to allow an escape from the situation into speculative thought. To this extent one may also say that dogmatics here meets the needs of preaching.

Nevertheless this does not mean that dogmatics simply fits in with the practical requirements of preaching, that the wish of the preacher becomes the father of the dogmatist's thought. Dogmatics does not submit to the needs of preaching, but together with preaching it submits to the demands of truth. It is basically the reflective aspect of preaching, it is a systematic reflection on the truth proclaimed by the preacher. It seeks to sum up and formulate, not as abstract doctrine but as the "norm" or "rule of faith", what for the preacher, conscious of his responsibilities, is the essential truth to be proclaimed. What in this connexion the dogmatist formulates, and what the preacher, following him, has to embody in the living word, namely the fact that man remains inescapably held in responsibility before God, is truth, the truth which emerges from encounter, the truth of God as regards human existence.

### 2. The New Existential Interpretation of the Doctrine of Original Sin

There follow two dogmatic themes in Questions 6 and 7. They are the two integrally connected themes of the *status integritatis* and of *the fall and original sin*.

From the point of view of preaching both these themes present the preacher with certain difficulties, but they must not be surrendered for that reason. The thought of the *status integritatis* is difficult because this human state is not provable empirically, psychologically or historically.

The fall and original sin are difficult because the doctrine of a quasi-physical inheritance of sin seems to be a downright contradiction of the essence of sin as guilt, of that very principle of responsibility which is so vital for preaching. The same applies to the thought that the pervasive corporate guilt of men of today is rooted in the guilty attitudes and conduct of their forbears. At this point the practical experience and sense of responsibility of the preacher suggests that some criticism should be made of the dogmatic tradition; and such criticism must take the form of new dogmatic insights and formulations. The doctrine of the fall and original sin can simply no longer be preached according to the traditional understanding of it. As preachers we cannot expect our hearers to accept it, because, after honest consideration, we must conclude that we ourselves are not prepared to accept it.

Perhaps it has never been possible truly to preach this doctrine. That it could have been established in its time by serious-minded theologians is probably rooted in the fact of a realistic (in the sense of the realism of universals) understanding of *natura humana*, according to which human nature, as something common to all men, i.e. humanity, formed a single real *concretum*, so that it was possible to conceive of the whole of humanity becoming guilty "in Adam". To what extent today it might be possible to renew this preparatory philosophical conception of the realism of universals is a question which cannot be further discussed here. In any event this realization of the philosophical background proper to the doctrine of original sin already takes us far beyond the current, traditional, popular conception of the doctrine. A criticism of this conception could be made in connexion with a discussion of philosophical realism.

To my mind it is clear that the growing criticism of the doctrine, which arises out of the preacher's sense of responsibility, will lead to a much deeper dogmatic insight into the truth which is at issue in the theological symbols of the fall of man and original sin. What is at issue in fact is the depth of the guilt in which the whole of humanity is involved. Sin, guilt in the sight of God, all real guilt in general, has, in consequence of the fact that humanity is tied up in one bundle of life, essentially the character of collective guilt. This point of view suggests something for preaching even in the traditional doctrine. It suggests that that doctrine contains a truth which in any event it is the preacher's duty to amplify, though perhaps this has been done hitherto on different lines.

If we wish rightly to evaluate the truth of this doctrine, after excluding interpretations that are impossible homiletically and dogmatically, we must start from the thesis that the story of the fall of man is not historical, nor even a part of saving history, but must rather be understood symbolically. (Furthermore, such a symbolic understanding, from a purely exegetic point of view, is not at all unsuitable to the literary character of Genesis 3 as an aetiological narrative.) We ourselves are Adam and Eve! Their disobedience is our disobedience. The pragmatics of temptation and guilt, so finely disclosed in this masterly narrative, is the pragmatics of our own temptation and guilt. (Thus Karl Barth with reference to the talking serpent: "The serpent really spoke, why, of course!" *Credo, Fragebeantwortung*, p. 164.) To this extent it may really be affirmed that in Adam the whole of human nature sinned. In this case however Adam is not simply Adam, a historical human being, or a figure in the drama of saving history, but ADAM, that is, man in general, the exponent of *natura humana*. And then guilt is from the outset to be qualified as the guilt of *natura humana*, hence not the guilt of individuals, but the guilt of all, collective guilt, plain guilt.

This being so, the answer to Question 7 ("Whence comes then such corruption in man's nature?") must not take the form of an allusion to the guilty conduct of our first parents, but rather of an allusion to the fact of guilt itself: man, ADAM, was indeed created by God for fellowship with Himself, and created therefore just and holy; yet he has rendered himself guilty in the sight of God. Created for life with God, he has preferred life without God. He wished to be himself as God and mistrusted God ("Did God say? . . ."). We put these sentences in the past tense. For man has always decided thus. He always finds himself entangled in this guilty situation, his existence is always implicated in it. The fall of man is in fact not a historical event, it is in a certain sense a "transcendental event". It did not take place at some particular time in the life-story of the individual (in childhood for instance or in a pre-existence). It is rather to be viewed as a falling away from God that is primaeval and original, conditioning all human existence, and which works out its effects, discloses itself, confirms itself in all concrete wrong conduct, whether of commission or omission.

This primaeval, original guilt, this desire to live apart from God, this desire to be as God, this mistrust of God, forms indeed the horizon of and is the pre-condition of all the personal responsibility and obligation which marks the individual life. And none the less (and this point does not contradict the former) it has a collective character. The individual, every individual, is interwoven into the bundle of guilt formed by the life of all. He is born into the guilt of all, into a human society which is enmeshed in radical guilt. He grows up in an atmosphere of wrong-doing and is inescapably caught in it; he grows into solidarity with the guilt which weighs on all.

Such is the pragmatics, the state of affairs springing from universal sinning, as formulated in the doctrine of original sin which we have now rightly understood. In this formulation, the idea of the physical inheritance of all-prevalent sin is replaced by the idea of social-moral solidarity at this point. Whereas the concept of a physical inheritance of sin obviously excludes and makes nonsense of the idea of personal responsibility, the pragmatics of sin makes room for both conceptions (and both in one)—the solidarity of all and the responsibility of the individual life. If it is understood in this way, the doctrine of original sin can once more stand up to the criticism which arises from the preacher's sense of responsibility. Thus we see that the criticism springing from the homiletic point of view has given birth to a fruitful new formulation in the field of dogmatics. Thus original sin can again be preached, and the doctrine can once more control preaching. For the hearer of the word of the preacher must be brought to the realization of his true situation before God by being referred to both factors—his personal responsibility as an individual and his solidarity with sinful humanity as a whole.

Understood thus, the doctrine not only can but must be faithfully maintained for the sake of preaching itself. We must under no circumstances surrender one jot of the doctrine of original sin. Otherwise we should be diluting the radicality of sin and belittling the honour of God, and both as theologians and preachers we should be failing in our duty to the one truth which has been revealed to us and which constitutes the essential content of all our discourse.

To dilute the notion of the radicality of sin would imply a belittling of the honour of God; for we have understood sin as life apart from God. If we make concessions at this point then we cast doubt on the radical nature of the truth that man as a matter of fact exists in separation from God. Thus God would cease to be the wholly Other, the One who dwells in transcendent majesty, exalted at an infinite height beyond man. He would become in a certain sense conformed to man, because man—if we surrender the conception of radical guilt—would have become in his possible piety and morality like unto God. God would in that case be a God whose essential demand actual empirical man could not only basically fulfil, but does in fact fulfil. If we preach on these lines, then we have ceased to proclaim the living God and His unapproachable glory. If we surrender the depth of human guilt in the eyes of God, then we also surrender the deep unfathomability and the ultimate mystery and hiddenness of the being of God.

There is of course a very well known type of preaching which adopts the style of undisturbing religious-moral exhortation, the style of the Sunday School lesson. This reassuring tone forgets and denies the glory of God; it renders human life innocuous and therewith it also renders God innocuous and undisturbing to man. But *this* God is no longer God, and such a type of preaching is easily and by far surpassed and outstripped in philosophy and poetry, is in fact outmatched by life itself with its peaks and its abysses. True preaching of the living God however must be a proclamation of truth that cannot be outstripped. Its secure basis, if it is to abide by the true glory of God and the right understanding of the being of God and of man, is the radical, "orthodox" approach to sin, undiluted and untainted by any touch of Pelagianism or Arminianism. On this account therefore preaching must be neither moralistic, nor legalistic, nor even pessimistic; it must take place with the full realization that natural man, in the heights and depths of his existence, exists in fact apart from God and therefore in sin and misery.

The kerygma of the living God and the kerygma of sin, rightly and radically understood, are correlates. The effect of the true understanding of sin is this—that the name of the living God does not become dissolved into a mere idea. That the name of the living God really evokes the living God of power and majesty is of course an event, vouchsafed by God Himself. Even when the right and essential understanding of sin dominates the point of view, it is still possible for preaching to be empty and lacking in vital inspiration, for it is possible that the event is still absent. The true dogmatic understanding of sin means that we do not from the outset refuse to surrender ourselves to the event, that we do not seek a refuge from the living God in the construction of a mere world-view. Thus in scripture God is encountered from the start as He who forgives sin, hence as the God who only in and with the recognition of human guilt is recognized by man as the true and living God. This is in fact to refer to the *name of God*: that name which He has given Himself. Let us compare the great pregnant text of Exodus 34:4ff.:

So Moses cut two tables of stone like the first; and he rose early in the morning and went up on Mount Sinai, as the Lord had commanded him, and took in his hand two tables of stone. And the Lord descended in the cloud and stood with him there, and proclaimed the name of the Lord. The Lord passed before him and proclaimed, "The Lord, the Lord, a God merciful and gracious, slow to anger, and abounding in steadfast love and faithfulness, keeping steadfast love for thousands, forgiving iniquity and transgression and sin, but who will by no means clear the guilty, visiting the iniquity of the fathers upon the children and the children's children, to the third and the fourth generation." And Moses made haste to bow his head toward the earth, and worshipped.

In this passage of scripture, the forgiveness of sins appears as a constitutive element in the name which God gives to Himself.

Secondly, if we surrender the doctrine of original sin and its all-prevalence, then the radicality of our understanding of sin is weakened. For to yield this doctrine, which establishes the common inescapable guilt in which all men are involved, would mean that in principle it might be demonstrated that, empirically, there have been, are, or will be, men who are free from sin and guilt. As contrasted with this, sin must be understood in such radical terms that it is impossible for any individual to escape from its entanglement. In such a situation a radically new beginning is needed: namely, the birth of the one sinless man through the divine incarnation.

Our new interpretation of the doctrine of original sin shows a quite specific movement of thought, which is probably typical of the creative criticism which arises when dogmatic work is strictly based on the needs and the task of the preacher: this movement of thought consists in a turning away from the successiveness which marks the conception of saving history to the structural interweaving of elements in an existential event which is existentially understood. Thus we have understood Genesis 3 to be a symbolical narrative, and hence we have understood the fall of man not as an event which initiates the process of saving history, but as symbolizing a transcendental basic

86

guilt which overshadows the individual in his solidarity with all. And likewise we have interpreted the all-prevalence of guilt, rightly posed by this doctrine, not as a matter of physical inheritance, hence not as a causal sequence, but as a matter of a solidarity from which there is no escape; hence as an existential structure.

The dogmatic structures, characterized by temporal sequences, which are engendered by the conception of saving history are unsuitable for the purpose of preaching. For the truth which the preacher has to proclaim is stamped by the character of immediate relevancy. (Even the ἐφ' ἅπαξ, the uniqueness, of the nativity of the God-man, the crucifixion and the resurrection, must in preaching be presented as something immediately relevant.) But the fall of man, understood in saving history as an initiatory event, could not be made of present relevance. But understood as transcendental guilt, indicating something basic and universal, it is relevant to the present moment of the individual life; the fall of man, presented in these terms, becomes something by which the individual can be challenged and his attention arrested. The fall then becomes a structural moment in the urgencies of the present situation. This understanding of truth as present relevancy—an understanding which arises from the situation by which the preacher is faced—must decisively shape dogmatic trains of thought. For only so can dogmatic formulations become the norm for the preacher, and enshrine that truth which in any event preaching is concerned to proclaim. (Here arises the question of the right understanding of time in theology.)

### 3. The "Status Integritatis"

This same principle of "present relevancy" must now also be brought to bear on the doctrine of the *status integritatis* which is likewise a component part of Question 6.

The idea of the *status integritatis* is necessarily connected with the thought of the fall in the current view proper to the conception of saving history, but it is equally so in the new understanding of the fall which we have just outlined. The very idea of man's guilt in the sight of God implies that it is something which God cannot have willed. (This is an analytical sentence!—The problem of the divine permission of sin, of divine influences in the lives of the godless, and of predestination, we shall leave for the present on one side.)

The theme of the *status integritatis* is kept firmly in view in Questions 6 and 7 of the Catechism. Naturally, as a result of our modified dogmatic understanding of original sin, the *status integritatis* can no longer be understood—as it is understood under the influence of the theory of saving history—as a paradisiacal state prior to the fall of man. For ourselves whose thought is orientated strictly by the requirements of the task facing the preacher the difficulty inherent in this idea lies, as has already been mentioned, in the fact that the *status integritatis* can in no way be shown to be, empirically, a real state of mankind. Yet if the thought is to have any dogmatic legitimation and relevance, in preaching, the hearer must be addressed in respect of his *status integritatis* and his attention must somehow be arrested in regard to this lost state. If the state is undemonstrable on psychological-empirical grounds, then there remains only the possibility that it belongs integrally to the demonstration which shows convincingly man's involvement in guilt; that the idea in a certain sense constitutes a structural moment in, or a vehicle of, such a demonstration.

Question 6 declares how man as a creature was willed and created by God. The affirmation includes the following Biblical and dogmatic themes: the *imago Dei* (man made in God's image): "true righteousness and holiness"; the knowledge of God, the love and praise of God; eternal blessedness and through all this, communion with God ("that man should live with God, praising Him for evermore").

The most comprehensive of all these themes and the basic feature which in fact underlies them all is the conception of communion with God. Through communion with God man expresses the reality denoted by the conception that he was made in God's image. And this communion implies concretely the knowledge, love and praise of God. In so far as man truly knows, loves and praises God, he is "objectively" truly righteous and holy, and from a "subjective" point of view he has real, indestructible, eternal felicity.

Preaching, however, can only challenge man and arouse his concern with regard to this original integrality of his being by showing him that it is something which he no longer possesses; by showing him that he does not live in communion with God, that he does not know, love and praise God, that therefore he has lost his true blessedness "subjectively" and that in consequence he stands before God "objectively" as one who is unrighteous and unclean (this in fact being true of man in the whole dimension of his being, in its whole span and richness, its heights and its depths); that therefore the "image of God" in him (thus understood) is destroyed. And this disclosure of man's utter failure to know, love and praise God, and of his consequent lack of felicity, can be so presented as to penetrate into the domain of empirical psychology, whence it will gain convincingness and striking power. This of course does not mean that it should be put forward as the result of an empirical-psychological survey of the facts. (Generally speaking it is perhaps true that we understand the psychological domain and its realities better, when we do not regard it as an autonomous domain enclosed in its own immanence, but as open rather to the transcendence of the Word of God. In this respect there would be room for a new "theological" psychology— the establishment of which can be shown to be an undeniable *desideratum* suggested by dogmatic work itself.)

In truth preaching can address man on the basis of the fact that, in all his striving for happiness, he does not in fact attain and enjoy happiness. The happiness which he supposes himself to have lacks substance and abiding worth. And it can so bring home to him these truths that he recognizes his image in the mirror it presents, it can convincingly show him that he does not know, love, and praise God. And man will have to attain this self-understanding in such a way as to understand at the same time and by implication that he ought to know, love, and praise God, that only by

89

so doing can he reach the full stature and fulfilment of his life. When man comes to understand this and thus truly to recognize his own condition in the sight of God, we have a type of understanding which, although including the psychological data (e.g. self-observation) leaves far behind it all understanding that remains on a purely psychological level. This is rather the kind of understanding and self-knowledge which springs from faith itself.

If we inquire how the continuity and interconnexion between dogmatics and preaching is illustrated at this point, it is that the dogmatic idea of the *status integritatis* provides the criterion, the standard of measurement, by which preaching assesses the true significance of man's actual present state, in order to convince him in consequence of his guilt before God. Sin could be given no better concrete illustration than that which is given, from a negative point of view, so to speak, in Question 6; here we realize, concretely, in what man's sinful situation consists. Thus far, this dogmatic thought presents with supreme clarity a regulative guide for preaching.

There follows then in consequence a second aspect of the doctrine of integrality, which really belongs to a different context of dogmatic thought: namely, the aspect of thankfulness and sanctification of life. The idea of the *status integritatis* becomes thus a pointer to the preaching of sanctification. The man who knows himself by faith to have been delivered by the grace of God and to be now a justified sinner, realizing too that he is actually not holy and just, will strive, out of thankfulness to the God who justifies the sinner, and under the deep conviction of His gracious reality, to embody true holiness and righteousness by ever-renewed decisions in the circumstances of his present life. He will strive to adumbrate, prefiguratively as it were, and at least by outline, the image of God in himself. Christian preaching must take account of this; it must be a preaching of sanctification.

The discussion of this point would be most appropriate in connexion with the third part of the Catechism, which treats of the ten commandments and the Lord's Prayer. The preacher's appeal for sanctification might however find its most outstanding canon in Question 6, in the doctrine of the *status integritatis*, which now becomes effective positively rather than negatively as a guide to preaching. From this point of view man can be shown towards what goal he has to strive, to what end he must make decisions, what is the essential, indeed the sole, purpose of his existence: namely, communion with God in the knowledge, love and praise of God. Here he comes to understand what purpose is served by the keeping of the commandments and the practice of prayer. Thus the *status integritatis* is both a guide and a standard in the process of sanctification.

### Theses developed in Chapter 5

16. In the interests of the truth of our understanding of God, there must be no surrender of the doctrine of original sin (Qu. 7). Just as little can we give up the radical understanding of sin (Qu. 8). The understanding of sin and the understanding of God are correlative. Questions 7 and 8 are strictly an explication of Question 1. (Cf. also on this point the considerations developed in chapter 6.)

17. Nevertheless for the sake of the genuineness and persuasive intelligibility of the preacher's address, the doctrine of the fall must not be taught in an objective way, under the influence of the theory of the saving process, as if it were a particular event in the history of humanity which, through physical inheritance, became the occasion of all subsequent sin. Rather what is implied by the fall of man is the transcendental basic guilt of every man, his inner estrangement from God regarded as the pre-condition of the possibility of his actual sinful thinking, speaking and doing. Furthermore in a rightly understood conception of original sin is contained the suggestion of a collective aspect of human guilt: the theme of the solidarity of mankind, of human society involved in an inextricable web of guilt.

18. The conception of the *status integritatis* (Qu. 6) raises a special problem for preaching in that its content is not demonstrable as a state of human life. Nevertheless it serves as a basis and canon for the preaching of sanctification.

CHAPTER 6

# THE RADICAL NATURE OF SIN AND THE ENSLAVED WILL

(Heidelberg Catechism Questions 8 and 9)

Question 8. "Are we then so depraved that we are utterly incapable of performing any good work and are inclined to all that is evil? Yes: unless it be that we are born again by the spirit of God."

Question 9. "Does not God then act unfairly by man, in that in His law He requires of him what he cannot perform? No; for God has so created man that he is capable of performing the good; but, by the instigation of the devil and through wilful disobedience, man has deprived himself and all his posterity of these gifts."

QUESTIONS 8 and 9 have again to do with objections which might weaken the radical nature of sin, and throw doubt on our obligation to assume the responsibility of guilt. "Are we then so depraved that we are utterly incapable of performing any good work and are inclined to all that is evil?" runs Question 8. Answer: Yes! But a qualification, one sole possible exception, is established: . . . "unless it be that we are born again by the Spirit of God". This exception or qualification is however bound up with a radical new beginning, with regeneration. Question 9 is concerned with an objection which tries to enable man to escape from the responsibility of guilt by invoking his incapacity (established by Question 5: "Can you keep this law perfectly? No . . ."); hence his *servum arbitrium*, his enslaved will. The reply of the catechism is that man in fact is in bondage as far as sin is concerned, but that he is also responsible for the loss of his freedom. The loss of freedom itself is an aspect of his sinful situation. God "does not act unfairly by man in that in His

92

law He requires of him what he cannot perform." For: "God has so created man that he is capable of performing the good; but, by the instigation of the devil and through wilful disobedience, he has deprived himself and all his posterity of these gifts."

### 1. *Existence as Radical Responsibility*

We enter here first on this latter theme, in connexion with Question 9: for preaching, inasmuch as preaching is the disclosure of the true human situation in the sight of God, two things are implied.

Firstly, it is affirmed that he who proclaims the gospel has to reckon with the enslavement of man to sin; on the other hand, however, he has none the less to convince man that he is reprehensible and guilty before God. These two things seem to be in contradiction with each other—only so, however, if we use a specific type of reflection about the problem of freedom, a type of reflection which is to be characterized as speculative. The whole treatment of the problem of freedom has no doubt long suffered from the speculative character of much of the discussion about it. Here again speculation consists in an attempt to escape from the hard facts of the situation. And this escape is effected by means of transferring without more ado to the whole of human existence certain relationships which may be studied and analysed somewhere within that sphere of man's daily life which lies within the ken of human understanding.

In the sphere of law, for example, it is the case that a person who has acted under compulsion, whether of persons or circumstances, hence not freely, cannot be made answerable for his deed: *Ultra posse nemo obligatur . . .* we are not responsible beyond "that which we are able". But if, without further consideration, we use this simple, obvious, analysable situation in daily life as an analogy to characterize existence as a whole, then we are rendering ourselves guilty of a *metabasis eis allo genos*—a change-over to something in a different category—and of a speculative flight from the ineluctable, inescapable obligations of existence. We are adapting existence as a whole (which is not at our disposal and does not lie within the field of man's power of comprehension and which, on the contrary, must be simply accepted as it is) to make it accord with some situation in the daily life of humanity which lies within our control and understanding. We are making something that transcends our control into something that is within the grasp of our thought. And it is just this which is called speculation! Since we have to accept existence as a whole—and the most characteristic thing about existence is that it just has to be accepted—the principle otherwise so evident, *ultra posse nemo obligatur*, does not apply here. Existence is by its very nature total and radical *obligatio*; we should fail to recognize its true nature, and we should be forgetting the most essential insight of the so-called philosophy of existence (which has its roots in Christian grounds) if we insisted on overlooking this basic character of existence.

Existence is an *obligatio* itself *ultra posse*. For we stand within existence itself, and not above it at some higher vantage point from which we might delimit certain parts of human reality as lying outside the sphere of *obligatio*, outside the inescapable necessity of accepting, hence outside the sphere of responsibility. Hence the existentialist thinker Sartre can declare that I am myself responsible for my life in every respect, in all its features, indeed even for the fact that I am alive at all (of course not in the juristic or ethical sense, but in the existential sense!); that for all this I have to be answerable. Any other point of view would have the effect of materializing existence and of disregarding its basic essential feature, namely, the obligation to accept total responsibility. Hence man cannot talk himself out of this situation by pleading the enslavement of his will, for he has to accept responsibility for this too. This was an insight common to the reformers as a whole, and it was reflected later in the statements of Question 9 of the Heidelberg Catechism. Without a doubt the point of view was a more appropriate, and more exact, description of the realities of man's existence in the face of God than that contained in the Pelagian or semi-Pelagian sequences of thought characteristic of a speculatively moulded scholasticism.

It is just at this point, in dealing with the problem of freedom, that there emerges the deep-seated difference between a legalistic-moral and an existential understanding of human life and its modes of behaviour. And it also becomes clear that the two points of view are not in competition; it is rather that the existential insight as the more comprehensive and inclusive is superior to, because more penetrating than, the other. The legalistic-moral point of view moves within a restricted sphere and finds its proper application only to specific phenomena, not to life as a whole. Only when the speculative mind elevates this derivative, secondary point of view into a sole, all-embracing criterion of life does a (false) competition arise. At the same time we must not overlook the fact that the basic thought in the existential view, the thought of responsibility, is maintained also within the outlook of the legalistic moralist, and in fact it alone makes his outlook possible.

Thus the legalistic-moral point of view has its roots deeply struck in the existential understanding of human life, and the latter finds an echo in the former. The thought of responsibility is the scarlet thread which runs through the reflections proper to both spheres. From this argument it follows that, as far as Christian proclamation is concerned, the preacher must in the first place seek to present and understand sin not on legalistic-moral lines, but on existential lines. On the other hand, however, it also follows that the basic existential situation is for the most part reflected in the legalistic-moral sphere, where, therefore, the preacher must trace and disclose its effects. (Our deep situation in the sight of God, namely, our lostness and unreality, is manifested pre-eminently in our refusal to face responsibility and in the lovelessness of our attitude towards our neighbour.)

Through the dogmatic perception and formulation of the truth that the human will is in bondage—the truth of the *servum arbitrium*—which is integral to the whole conception of sin, and for which man is himself responsible, Christian proclamation will gain a renewed understanding of sin's radical nature. Sin which does not imply the enslavement of the will is not sin at all in the true sense. A Pelagian understanding of sin, which regards the wickedness in man as something which may be overcome by good intention and strong resolution, fails to perceive the depth of human misery and in very truth is no longer speaking of the same thing. In such a point of view it is not sin, but the badness of man from the moral angle, which occupies the centre of the picture. A simple, optimistic moralism and perfectionism might here find a place in edificatory discourse. However, once we begin to enquire, first on purely empirical-psychological lines, into the deep basis for the moral perversity of mankind, when we proceed from the morally reprehensible actions and words to the thoughts and impulses, the inner dispositions and affections, when at that point we suddenly find ourselves faced by the bottomless abyss of the incalculable falsity and depravity of the human heart, then we gain the deep conviction that such a moralistic, edificatory point of view is inadequate to the realities of the situation. Then the question strikes us forcibly: what is sin essentially and at bottom?

In such a case, beginning with the straightforward lines of empirical-psychological observation and reflection, we find that we have in fact pierced the level of the Pelagian-moralistic point of view and have struck a new and far deeper level of thought. Thus a simple moralism becomes discredited by the consideration of the ethical-psychological realities of life itself, in all their complexity, their far-reaching implications, the deep problematics they pose, and our vision is then open to the question of sin in all its radicality. Morality is a universally given phenomenon, it is a necessarily social phenomenon. But moralism, a moralistic outlook on life, or an inner moralistic attitude, is disingenuous inasmuch as it serves to conceal, in very truth, the ultimate depths of being.

It need hardly be said that the Church's proclamation of Jesus Christ cannot possibly move on such a superficial level of thought. The discourses of Jesus Himself, with their onslaught against the legalism of the Pharisees, in fact the whole manifestation of truth in Jesus Christ, points us in a different direction, a direction in which the deeper reality to which we have referred becomes illuminated. The narrowly legalistic, moralistic, position and preaching and personal attitude adopted in certain church circles injuriously affects therefore the Church's fulfilment of its true mission. It does not win men for the gospel. It repels them, and where it does win men over—and this is said humanly speaking, and with the express reservation of the free efficacious working of the Holy Spirit—it wins them for something other than the gospel. It is adapted to conceal from contemporary human society the real issues at stake.

## 2. The "Servum Arbitrium" and the Problem raised by the Concept of Freedom

To summarize now our argument so far: we have seen that the objection with which Question 9 deals is not a valid objection in that, by drawing a falsely analogical conclusion, it effects a *metabasis eis allo genos*, a change to something on a different plane—from the legalistic-moral plane of thought to the existential plane—whereas in fact these two planes are to be strictly distinguished since the types of thought to which they give rise show a basically different structure. The structures of the secondary and subordinate plane may not be simply transferred to the deep and original one.

The basis from which the argument against the true doctrine of original sin proceeds is assailable from two sides. For the argument presupposes the alternative: either sin is surmountable by the free decisions of the will, or it is not: if not, then man cannot be made answerable for it. Two objections are to be raised against this alternative: if sin is regarded as surmountable by the free decisions of the will, then, following a Pelagian mode of thought, its radical character is disregarded. If however the enslavement in which sin takes place is viewed as dispensing man from responsibility, then the whole character of human life as a radical *obligatio*, compelling acceptance of responsibility, is ignored. In any event therefore the argument falls to the ground in that it either disregards or does not take seriously the essential character of that which is in question.

As far as preaching is concerned, we learn from these considerations that it must abide by the real character of human existence and avoid all such deviously speculative modes of thought which undeniably miss the real point at issue.

We have already opposed to the alternative presupposed by this invalid argument the antithesis implied in reformation thought, which again is two-pronged (and the acceptance of this dual position, like the previous dual denial of the false antithesis, is obligatory in preaching): on the one hand, sin occurs without any free decision; we no longer enjoy the *posse non peccare*, the ability not to sin; on the other hand, however, man is none the less responsible for his sin.

Now the two principles of this reformation antithesis, as has already been intimated, can be summed up in one single affirmation: namely, that the loss of freedom represents an integral element, a structural moment, in sin itself. Man sins, not of his own free will; he acts, thinks, and speaks under compulsion (not *coactio* but *necessitas*!); he is now utterly deprived of the possibility of not sinning. But the fact that he has lost this possibility and this freedom is the very essence of sin. And just as we have re-interpreted Question 6, with its doctrine of the fall, by transferring it from the type of thought arising from the concept of saving history to a transcendental-existential type of thought, so we must proceed similarly with the answer to Question 9: "God has so created man that he is capable of performing the good; but, by the instigation of the devil and through wilful disobedience, man has deprived himself and all his posterity of these gifts."

Here there is a clear allusion to the disobedience of the

archetypes of humanity, Adam and Eve. Thus Question 9 coheres with Question 6: the essential consequence of the fall and original sin is none other than just the loss of this freedom. And now, consistently with our more appropriate re-interpretation of the fall, this loss of freedom cannot have taken place once for all, at one specific moment in the history of humanity, whence it has worked out its causal consequences for all later generations: rather it belongs, as an essential moment, as a transcendental prior condition of the possibility of sinning, to the sin of every individual. In the experience of every individual the fall of man basically occurs, and therewith the loss of original freedom. As we have already said, the fall of man is the transcendental elemental catastrophe, entailing guilt and therewith the transcendental loss of freedom. All actual sins, whether in thought, word or deed, are rooted in the basic fact that man can do none other than sin, because he has already and universally renounced his freedom to live unto God.

This re-interpretation of the loss of freedom flowing from the re-interpretation of the fall and original sin brings us up against the problem arising from the whole concept of freedom. In what does freedom really consist? Whoever has understood the phenomenon of sin, whoever apprehends sin phenomenologically in all its radicality, will understand too that no man can sin deliberately, by free choice. Even he who "is determined to play the villain", like Richard III, or who, despite a last appeal to change his mind, persists obstinately, impenitently and consciously in his sin, like Don Juan, is not acting freely. Whosoever sins is always the slave of sin. And it is precisely in such extremist figures, who deliberately will evil, that the daemonic overwhelming might of sin which holds humanity in its grip becomes still more manifest. The essence of sin consists precisely in enslavement.

But what then is freedom, if no one can sin by free choice? Freedom is obviously only possible as freedom to do the good, as freedom to live unto God. This is the Augustinian concept of freedom which in our days has been especially re-emphasized by Karl Barth. According to this conception, freedom is not the pure indifference of a *liberum arbitrium*— a will that is free—of a capacity to do thus or otherwise; it is not an empty concept, it is essentially something which is akin to fulfilment. No doubt it always means freedom from . . . but it also means in consequence freedom for the accomplishment of something. Not freedom that spells indifference, but freedom to live unto God. Since freedom of this kind has been lost, since man is always and everywhere enmeshed in estrangement from God, and is hence involved in a situation implying the loss of freedom, actual sin occurs.

This estrangement from God, this original loss of freedom to live unto God, hence transcendental, metaphysical guilt, is the always-given basic datum which underlies all actual human conduct. This given basic datum is not something that can be established and observed on empirical lines. It transcends the empirical. The fact that man is a sinner in the sight of God is something which lies beyond all psychology. Nevertheless, this givenness, this original metaphysical guilt is of such a kind that it enables us the better to understand in their depths the empirical existing facts of human life, which in spite of everything can be observed and established by psychological means. We have in fact just given an example of the deeper appreciation of psychological realities through the idea of sin by showing that mere moralism founders simply by the consideration of moral phenomena in all their implications.

But of what nature then is this transcendental metaphysical guilt, this original alienation from God, seeing that it transcends the empirical-psychological factors and remains none the less in close relation to them, enabling us to perceive and appreciate them the better? We might be tempted to speak in this connexion of a hypothesis. Yet to do so would merely shift the ground of the problem. Transcendental, metaphysical guilt is no working hypothesis constructed to give us a better understanding of psychological phenomena. Hypotheses belong to the realm of theory. Here we are confronted by something eminently practical. Transcendental, metaphysical guilt, although not psychologically observable, is nevertheless in a certain sense a factor in man's experience. It falls within our experience in fact in the necessity of decision, on the basis of self-understanding, in the depths of the responsible personality, which feels compelled to accept its load of guilt in the presence of God. For if the original turning away from God were merely a hypothesis, if it did not fall within human experience, then it would not be possible to preach about it. But it is something which is preached about; preaching must again and again address man on the basis of this his basic underlying estrangement from God, must attempt to bring it home to him as the truth which is reflected in his concrete sinful conduct.

Only through this ultimate truth can the sinful conduct of man be qualified as sinful. Apart from the realization of it, apart from the appreciation of the true basic fall of man, all talk of sin remains empty phrases, a discourse which continues to run on the lines of an effete tradition, no longer vitally understood. And if the talk of sin is reduced to the possible actual sins that may be in view, then the preacher once more ends up in sheer moralism. Sin is then no longer a turning away from the person of the living God; it is no more than a violation of a human moral system. Such violation is then pathetically and unjustifiably called sin, and God perhaps becomes no more than the exponent and guarantor of a violated human system of morals, to defend which He is invoked.

Since we are now speaking of the possibility of experiencing transcendental guilt in the depths of the responsible personality, we stand confronted by the whole mystery of human personality, of human being in responsibility. This gives an intimation of itself firstly in the fact that personal life and its experience in the acceptance of responsibility can be observed on empirical psychological lines, secondly in the fact that nevertheless it leaves this level far behind and reaches down to much deeper bases, as it were; that therefore there is for us a thoroughly accessible, vividly apprehensible psycho-physical reality (which does not mean "bodily") falling within our experience, which nevertheless eludes in its ultimate essence all power of observation. The ultimate element of our analysis lies not in the sensuous and observable but in the self; but the "self" is transcendent as something that cannot be objectivized, it eludes the approach of any sort of "method".

Freedom in its deepest essence is at home here in this deepest stratum of the mysterious personality. We have dissolved the current notion of freedom as *liberum arbitrium*, the will that is free, by appeal to the far more tenable, richer, conception of Augustine. Naturally, however, the former notion of freedom has also its part to play and its proper justification, that is, in the legalistic and possibly in the moral sphere. For example, we have the freedom to conclude an agreement or not, and if we conclude an agreement in such freedom, without any sort of compulsion, then it is legally valid. Hence we find in this context of thought the same situation as we have already met earlier; namely, the situation in which a notion proper to and thoroughly intelligible in the legalistic-moral sphere is transferred to existence as a whole, to the origins and depths, and used to qualify personal being as a whole, thus producing a confusion of understanding. In the case of the *liberum arbitrium* we are faced not by a wrong idea of freedom, but by an idea of freedom which belongs to a different order of life and level of thought. The Augustinian notion of freedom, however, which we have contrasted with the latter as the truer and more original, has of course not solved the problem of freedom—probably one of the most difficult problems for thought that exist and as vexing for the theologian as for the philosopher—but it has none the less taken us further. If any one really understood the Augustinian idea of freedom, and the full meaning of freedom for the good, freedom for God, then he would probably have understood the whole mystery. I do not scruple to affirm that this is properly an object for meditation, for mystical contemplation at the deepest level. Nor does this exclude further intellectual clarification.

### 3. *The Loss of Freedom as Transcendental, Metaphysical Guilt*

Finally a notion which we have used many times must now be the object of special clarification. We have described the original loss of freedom, the real heart and centre of sin, the act whereby man adopts an attitude towards God of such a kind that he can do no other but sin, as transcendental primal guilt. We have also characterized our re-interpretation of the current understanding of the story of the fall (derived from the concept of saving history) as transcendental. In our context of thought what is the meaning of the Kantian idea of the transcendental? To what extent is it really applicable and appropriate?

In the thought of Kant "transcendental" means the condition governing the possibility of something. (This is not the same thing as the cause of something!) The transcendental condition underlying possibility is implanted in man. It might be called *cum grano salis* a "capacity" or a *facultas* of man. It is a condition governing the possibility of acts, as for example the act of knowledge or recognition. For instance, the fact that I am in a position to establish chains of causation in reality, or rather, that the whole of reality necessarily imposes itself on me as a causal sequence, is according to Kant transcendentally conditioned by the category of causality which inheres in my reason. This category is already implanted within me, and makes possible the particular acts in which I observe causal sequences. This shows clearly that the fact of something being already and always intrinsic to my mind is the really characteristic note of the transcendental. The transcendental conditioning of possibility is not some one among a series of acts. It is something which transcends particular acts, which lies behind them; it is always and already inherently effective in making such acts possible.

Now we have explained with regard to the fall and original

sin, that it is not something which once took place in the
process of saving history and in the history of man; nor is it
a biographical event in the life of each individual, occurring
at some time in earliest childhood or perhaps in some sort
of pre-existence, and then working out its consequences for
everything that comes later. The fall, the primal guilt, the
turning away from God, the loss of freedom, is no doubt
an act; but it is not an act which, historically or biographi-
cally demonstrable, has taken place once for all (when in
fact could it have taken place?) but an act which has always
already taken place, in short a "transcendental act". The
Kantian idea of the transcendental characterizes fairly
accurately the essential feature of what we have in mind
and is so far appropriate. I am always already in a state of
estrangement from God, and in every act of sin which I
recognize and regret as such, this prior condition of my
being strikes me with renewed force. And precisely when we
characterize the fall and original sin, the primal guilt, as
loss of freedom, does its transcendental nature become
especially manifest. For each sinful deed takes place in a
state of bondage because the sinner has already and always
lost his freedom; and that is so, not through one particular action which initiates the series of all other acts of effective sin, but through one transcendental act which lies
behind and governs the whole series of particular acts, and
which does not take place at some time or other but which
always takes place, or rather, which has always already
taken place.

For preaching, this transcendental pattern of thought is of
particular importance because it produces an interlocking
of two things, the perceptible and the imperceptible; and
this inter-connexion is for the preacher, in a certain sense, a
vital necessity. The transcendental pattern of thought
implies the psychologically perceptible aspect of sin. But
it does not permit the preacher to remain at this stage. For
if he did so, he would not be really talking about sin. Sin
in its essence is the turning away from God. This however
is not something which is psychologically perceptible. But

it stands in the closest connexion with the psychologically perceptible aspect of sin, as its basic transcendental condition. Were it to be viewed in isolation, apart from this connexion, then the whole thing would become a matter of phrases and theory. The transcendental pattern of thought secures, in regard to sin, that interconnexion of the perceptible and that which lies beyond perception, which is a vital necessity for true proclamation. It is therefore clearly in this matter the appropriate dogmatic formulation of an essential theme of preaching. Thus the preacher can address man at one and the same time on the basis of his clearly perceptible conduct in this world and his ulterior, imperceptible relation to God.

### 4. *The Radical Understanding of Sin and Ethics*

After discussing the concept of freedom and the *servum arbitrium* we have to deal with the other objection (already mentioned) to the radicality of the orthodox doctrine of sin, and to consider also the answer given to it in Question 8. "Are we then so depraved that we are utterly incapable of performing any good work and are inclined to all that is evil?" Answer: "Yes; unless it be that we are born again by the Spirit of God."

The objection calls in question the radical nature of sin. The answer holds fast to it. The objection must be of special concern to us in relation to the pattern which we have posed. For it has its starting point and its support in the realm of the empirical, of the psychologically observable, in that realm therefore which we must not leave out of account in our preaching. When now we examine what in fact confronts us in our daily experience of life, can we honestly talk in such a blunt and audacious manner about a radical sinfulness inherent in the human race, so that man "is incapable of performing any good work and is inclined to all that is evil"? Are we not thus falling into an orthodoxy that is remote from actual life, hence unintelligible and unconvincing, and hence an orthodoxy for which the preacher cannot be expected to be answerable? Does not life rather bear the appearance of a mixture of good and bad in humanity, on the one hand a mixture of good and bad elements in human society, and again, a mixture of good and bad in the human heart itself, a picture which suggests rather an ever enduring struggle of the good against the evil? Ought we not rather as honest preachers of the gospel to respect human reality as we in fact find it to be and to see clearly and say clearly that good is good and bad is bad?

In truth the gradations and the discriminations which we are conscious of in our psychological and sociological experience must be taken into account in our preaching also and not denied. Otherwise there arises an almost frivolous talk about sin, a briskly pious, uncriticized, and hence in the last resort flippant canting about "We are all of us sinners. . . . !", which then is quite rightly not understood and simply not believed. There is a kind of disregard of experienced reality in preaching, the effect of which is to leave the hearer unconvinced. When the preacher is compelled to declare, by the inspiration and exigencies of his theme, the opposite of what seems to be obvious, then he must do so with understanding of, and not in disregard of, reality as men have experienced it and may experience it.

And such an understanding of and respect for reality must be of an existential kind; it must spring from the preacher's own experience and serious approach to life; the preacher himself must stand within our common human reality, he must be solicited and assailed by it. A preaching about the divine meaning granted to life without the preacher being in any way aware of the threatening meaninglessness of everything earthly, a preaching about the forgiveness of sins without the preacher having any suspicion of the distress of sin, a preaching about the foolishness of the cross without the preacher having any thoughts about the wisdom of this world, is necessarily unconvincing. No doubt in this connexion the hesitations and doubts suggested by life itself may have been understood and experienced as something triumphantly overcome: but they must have been understood and experienced. . . . The preacher must know himself intimately, he must grapple with his own experience of life, he must realize his own dimensions and limits. This will prevent him from preaching otherwise than from the depths of his own personal understanding of life, his own personal struggle with doubt, and hence it will prevent him from preaching disingenuously.

Further examples could be given. And yet in any event there must be sounded in all this the note of radical and universal sin, which simply wipes out the discriminations of a moralism based on psychological and sociological grounds.

And just at this point, in full awareness of the empirically manifest situation, the preacher must preach a truth, a reality, which clashes with appearance. Even in face of the real distinctions between men, in face of the whole range of the *humanum* which stretches from the criminal to the saint, we must declare to be valid without reservation the doctrine: "We are all of us sinners and utterly fail to reach that righteousness which alone has value in the eyes of God. . . ." Do we not see in human society and in the individual man a mixture of good and evil? "Are we then so depraved that we are utterly incapable of performing any good work and are inclined to all that is evil?" The answer is "Yes". The preacher must be fully aware of what he is saying when he says this. But his realization of the complexities of human life must not prevent him from saying it. Otherwise the way would be open for man to save himself by his own efforts. In that case it would simply be a matter of striving, in social as in individual life, to see that the mixture was constantly being changed in favour of the good, until finally all evil was rooted out. Even were it to be objected that this ideal could never be perfectly attained, that there would always be a remnant of evil, we should have to reply that on this view it would be possible in principle, as is shown by the real moral differences in men, and that in view of such constant progress the surviving traces of evil would no longer signify much. In any case such surviving evil would not suffice to yield evident and adequate grounds for the wholesale reprobation of humanity.

Thus in this matter any other view but that of the orthodox doctrine of sin leads to the possibility of man's salvation of himself by his own efforts, hence to the negation of what is formulated in the first question and answer of the Catechism as the central kerygma. Thus would be denied the radicality and inescapability of confrontation by God, and in fact we should be denying the being of God Himself. For in Question I encounter with God is defined as being under a debt to that Other from whom I can receive myself back only as a total person. So here in the answer which must be given to Question 8 there must lie the proof of what in the opening of this essay we set forth as the essential characteristic of all dogmatics and preaching, namely, that they have solely to explicate what is implied in genuine encounter with God.

Everything is already contained in the opening of the Catechism: and in having to decide on an answer to Question 8, which does not cancel out the truth expressed in Question I, but rather confirms it, we have therefore not contented ourselves with issuing some arid postulate as irrefragable, to which everything, if necessary with violence, would have to be adjusted; we have simply and solely unfolded in terms of conceptual thought the fullness and richness of the one needful encounter with God. This original unity of the religious consciousness does not permit us to teach and preach about sin otherwise than is indicated in Question 8.

Then it becomes still clearer in view of the gradations established by moralism that man, as Question 8 has it, is universally and radically enmeshed in sin, which is not a merely moralistic qualification. Even the man who, according to human standards, is truly virtuous, is in truth, at the heart of his existence, "incapable of performing any good work and inclined to all that is evil". He too in his inner dispositions, and the behaviour which results from them, is through and through determined by the transcendental primal guilt, the original turning away from God and the consequent loss of freedom to live unto God. He too therefore is utterly dependent on the "one sole comfort in life and death", on Him who "with His dear blood has fully paid the ransom price for my sins and delivered me from the power of the devil". Unless this one truth is realized, man is concealing from himself his deepest and therefore his true situation in the sight of God.

Let the preacher consider well what he has to say in this context of thought! Then he will no longer think slightingly of sin and forgiveness, nor, preaching reluctantly on the theme, make it appear of trivial importance. Even the virtuous man is held under the law of sin, and therefore exists in unreality in the eyes of God. Perhaps the very terms of the Heidelberg formula will help us to a better appreciation of the truth in this matter. We are *"incapable* of performing any good work, and *inclined* to all that is evil". In other words, man is still incapable of performing any *truly* good work, even when he does what is morally good; he remains inclined to all evil, even when he avoids evil and behaves virtuously. Accordingly the moral good which man does is not in truth the good, because, even while doing it, he remains inclined to evil.

The inclination to evil disqualifies even the good which he actually does; and this is fully true as soon as we think of man's situation as it exists in the sight of *God*. The good cannot then count as the truly good in the eyes of God; it cannot be "reckoned to man as righteousness". Morally bad conduct and morally bad dispositions are no doubt in any case a sympton of man's radical unrighteousness in the sight of God; but in this context of thought the reverse is not true. There is of course morally good conduct among men; there is also morally good character and disposition, especially in the field of social relations, manifesting itself as a certain observable faithfulness in the behaviour of human beings towards each other. In the sight of God, however, no man's inner disposition is good.

Hermann Friedrich Kohlbrugge writes in his *Elucidatory and Confirmatory Questions concerning the Heidelberg Catechism"*: "Why does the Catechism ask: 'Are we then so depraved . . . etc.'? Answer: Firstly, because we do not cease to entertain a good opinion and conceit of ourselves.

Secondly, to bring us to the conviction that we are in truth lost creatures, however worthy, pious and honest we may be, so long as we are not born again of God. Thus the realization of our misery must drive us to seek new life from God . . ." The contrary to the unreality, the unrighteousness in the sight of God, which inheres even in him who is morally good so far as his fellow men are concerned, is therefore the "being born again of God", the enjoyment of "fullness of life flowing from God". Wherever this is not, then man lives in unreality, missing the mark of his true calling, and as a "rotten tree" he can only bring forth evil fruits, however much the morality of outward behaviour is observed.

"Life from God, life in God" is however something that clearly implies a personal relationship; it signifies a personal tie, personal obligation, personal communion. Outside this sense of communion man cannot but be a creature existing in unreality, existing falsely and superficially. All the concrete happenings, the whole of the observable conduct of his life, is essentially qualified by this basic factor. How then could we suppose that—provided man is really created for communion with God—outside this relationship he could live other than falsely and superficially, other than as a lost soul? How could we accept that, where this relationship, decisive for existence, is disturbed, man could be capable of any sort of true good, of anything in fact, any word, deed or thought, which might bring his being nearer to its true fulfilment?

To be sure, the assertion that all men are morally of little worth is simply not true. And the preacher must not take refuge in such an untrue assertion in order to rescue the Biblical and dogmatic idea of the radicality of sin! Hence it may indeed be the case that for him who is accustomed to think in moralistic categories, and who remains faithful to them, the orthodox talk about the depth and universality of sin will seem repulsive and incomprehensible. On the other hand it might also seem incomprehensible to a man that one should succeed, by talk about duty and worth and virtue, in concealing the deep lostness of all humanity. The awareness of the latter rests not on a pessimistic but on a realistic view of life. From the story of the fall and original sin there speaks forth more and deeper wisdom than from any moralistic anthropology.

The task of the preacher is to hold fast to this insight in all integrity and consistency. For this purpose however the answer to Question 8, viewed as a strict explication of Question 1, must somehow find confirmation also in the sphere of experience. Otherwise the great danger is that dogma remains dogma and nothing else. The preacher must dare to show that "all our doings are nothing worth", even in the best life. He must bring home to his hearers the truth that they themselves—even with all their rectitude and moral virtue—are really in the position of the prodigal son. He must preach in such a way that this truth strikes forcibly and convincingly the mind of the highly respectable man himself. Therefore he may use the immorality which ever confronts him, in the souls of his hearers, in his own heart also, and in the surrounding world, as an example to illustrate his theme, but never as a means of proof. Sin must be preached about in such a way that none can go home and except himself from the general condemnation—unless it be *per nefas*, wrongfully, by which means he is judging himself before God—but not *per fas*, legitimately, in that the sermon was so presented as to make this excepting of oneself quite allowable.

This disclosure of the universality of sin, so presented that none can regard himself as outside its scope, may become effective in various ways. The preacher for example may try to show from the example of the individual life (as much as possible from experience) how even righteous and morally respectable action can conceal within it a root of the evil, loveless disposition which poisons everything. Compassion, for example, as Nietzsche so shrewdly pointed out, can so often imply a hidden striving for power. Again there is the impulse to self-exaltation sometimes behind the apparently humblest self-abasement ("Whoever humbles himself, the same *shall* be exalted"). Or again he may point to the hard core of Pharisaism which may secretly accompany upright, respectable action and character. In all this, however, we must realize that it is not our mission to cast doubt, in our preaching, on decency and uprightness as such, and to bring these virtues under general suspicion and condemnation. In this respect our discourse should not be categorical, but rather illustrative in character.

Another way of bringing home the inescapability of sin is to use Bultmann's well-known train of thought: that every good work, in so far as it does not spring from faith itself, is *eo ipso* sinful, because it is performed in the secret consciousness of one's own goodness and therefore implies a καυχᾶσθαι before God, a claim on the part of man to justify himself. It is not only because man does not fulfil the law of God, that he is a sinner and stands in need of grace; but even though he perfectly fulfilled the law and thus supposed himself no longer to be in need of grace, he would be still more a sinner. This thought, with which Bultmann claims to pierce the inner motives in the life of Paul, again reflects the idea of transcendental primal guilt, it points to the deep-rooted wrongness in the relation of both unmoral and moral man towards God.

We find a third way in Calvin (*Inst.* I, 1):

So long as we do not look beyond this earth, we can be fully content with our own righteousness, wisdom and virtue, and we flatter ourselves hugely that we are very near to being demi-gods! But if we once begin to direct our thoughts upwards to God, when we begin to consider what kind of God He is, when we ponder the strict perfection of His righteousness, wisdom and goodness, then what previously dazzled our eyes under the illusory garb of righteousness, now takes on the appearance of the most terrible unrighteousness; what made a wonderful impression on us as wisdom now becomes horribly manifest as the most wicked folly; what wore the mask of virtue now stands disclosed as the most pitiable weakness. So little can what seemed the best conduct among us men stand before the purity of God.

A fourth way lies in the invocation of the example of Jesus Christ, the one sinless man (Heb. 4:15) who in His sinlessness, in the perfection of His surrender to the Father, demonstrates to us what can be the full stature of man devoted wholly to God. Of course this sinlessness of the man Jesus of Nazareth is not something that we should attempt to demonstrate on historical lines; it results rather, in a certain sense, from the postulate of faith in the total appearance of Jesus Christ as the appearance of the incarnate God Himself.

All these means or examples enabling us concretely to show the inescapability of sin have one feature in common: they bring home to man, and to the morally "good" man also, the fact that he is a sinner, inasmuch as they confront him with the living God. Sin stands disclosed in the light of the command of Jesus: "You, therefore, must be perfect, as your heavenly Father is perfect" (Matt. 5:48). As soon as man ceases to live thoughtlessly alone with himself and the world which surrounds him, as soon as he becomes aware of God as the one true possibility governing his being, he can no longer regard himself as anything other than lost and wretched in the sight of God. And the blame for this he can ascribe not to God, but to himself alone. The recognition of the true God is always accompanied by the recognition of one's own apartness from God. Otherwise it would not be a recognition of the true God. Thus the man who comes to know God comes to know at the same time his own sin and misery. That pair of ideas (which have become alive for us above all through the work of dialectical theology), namely "judgment and grace" denotes the manner or way of all true knowledge of God. A (as it were) neutral knowledge of God, untouched by this thought, a knowledge of God in the sense of "natural theology", just does not exist. It would stand in contradiction to the very "idea" of God.

Thus then for preaching there is a way from the proclamation of sin to the proclamation of God which at the best is very conditioned; on the other hand the awareness of sin flows necessarily from the right proclamation of God.

### 5. *The Works of the Regenerate*

Finally, in the context of this consideration of the radicality and universality of sin, there is yet a problem which we must briefly touch upon: that of the new birth unto righteousness. According to Question 8 we are "incapable of performing any good work and are inclined to all that is evil", "unless it be that we are born again by the Spirit of God". As has been already said, this decrees an exception to the universality and radicality of sin: the exception lies in the conduct and disposition of the regenerate.

The man who has been born again by the Spirit of God clearly thinks and acts not in wickedness but in goodness. What sort of meaning are we to attach to this exception? It is clear that with the posing of this question we find ourselves already in the third part of the Catechism. Therefore, according to our interpretation of Question 2 we are here concerned with the third aspect of Christian preaching, where it is a question of man's thankfulness, of the concrete living of the Christian life and of the appeal which Christian preaching has to make in this respect. To what extent can the striving and endeavour of the regenerate man be described as "good" and not "bad", when he seeks to fulfil the will of God by the keeping of the commandments, and is concerned by the practice of prayer to give glory to God? Is such a man transformed mentally and emotionally so that from an empirical psychological point of view he may be with certainty distinguished from the "natural man"?

We may not talk about the life of the regenerate in this way, because sin itself, from the grip of which he has obviously broken free, is no datum that is empirically observable and demonstrable. Rather is it true that the dialectic of Romans 7:14ff. applies also, and precisely, to the existence of those who have been born again. The preacher must hold fast to this truth if he is not to become unrealistic in his preaching. And that the Catechism cannot have interpreted the new life of the Christian in any other sense is shown by Question 60, among others: "How are you just before God?" The answer is: "Solely through true faith in Jesus Christ", and it is firmly added that "my conscience accuses me of having grievously sinned against all the commandments of God, and of never having kept any of them, and warns me that I am still ever inclined to all that is evil". Similarly Question 114, after explaining the ten commandments, goes on: "Can however those who have turned again to God perfectly observe these commandments?" "No, but even the most holy, so long as they are in this life, have only made a small beginning in the way of this obedience; yet with serious purpose they have begun to live, not according to a few only, but according to all the commandments of God."

Thus, if we follow the Catechism, disobedience and the inclination to all evil *remain* in the regenerate! None the less the striving and the endeavour of the regenerate man is qualified as good. Hence this qualification is not an empirical one; it is valid, rather, in the sight of God. In the sight of God the good works of those who have been born again are reckoned as good. But they are not good in themselves: ". . . even our best works in this life are all imperfect, and stained with sins . . ." (Qu. 62).

The primal sin, the turning away from God, which underlies both moral and immoral actions, is not suspended. But it persists as something that has been forgiven. For good works are now works of the believer. They are performed in the consciousness of forgiveness. The consciousness of forgiveness is integral to all the aspirations and endeavours of the regenerate. And because forgiveness is the inspiring reality in the life of the believer, because it is operative and efficacious, the works done in the consciousness of it are qualified as good works. Not for their own sake, not because of their intrinsic quality—for in regard to basic emotions and mental make-up the regenerate man cannot be distinguished in principle from the "natural man"—but in virtue of divine forgiveness. God Himself gives to the endeavours of the regenerate man for the sake of the forgiveness which inspires them, and of which the man is fully conscious, a different qualification. This fact, the new qualification which God grants, is intimated for example in Question 63, which speaks about the reward of good works: "But do our good works deserve nothing, does not God will to reward them in this and the future life?" "Such reward is not granted because of their merit, but by grace."

If we view matters in this light we shall not lose contact with empirical-psychological realities in our preaching about regeneration and forgiveness, nor, on the other hand, shall we be pressed into the impossible assertion that there is a qualitative difference, psychologically, in the regenerate Christian. Good works are of no avail, that is to say, they deserve no reward, and yet on the other hand they have a meaning. What is this meaning? The answer must be: that they adumbrate and prefigure the realization of the Kingdom of God and its eschatological righteousness. The good works of the Christian do not actually bring the Kingdom of God on earth, but God wills such works as signs and tokens and allows them validity as such.

Because in this way we do not lose contact with the empirical-psychological level of thought, the proclamation of this theme has the possibility of making an appeal which otherwise would be lost. Thus far the true understanding of the exception to the universality and radicality of sin which stems from the experience of regeneration is of the greatest significance for our preaching. When he assimilates the thought of "ethical adumbration" (without any claim to merit), the preacher can and must echo with a good conscience and in all earnestness that call of Jesus: "You, therefore, must be perfect, as your heavenly Father is perfect."

### Theses developed in Chapter 6.

19. Although the preacher, with Question 8, must be faithful to the thought of the radical nature of sin, he must not leave out of account the empirically observable moral gradations and differences among men, if his preaching of sin and judgment is not to become disingenuous. Sin may not be preached about in moralistic terms as the transgression of laws and ordinances; otherwise the preaching about sin deteriorates into a preaching about morals, and the morally good man can legitimately elude its challenges. The reality of sin as transcendental primal guilt

is not apprehensible in its depths on the plane of moralistic thought. Although man must be addressed by the preacher with regard to the observable level of moral conduct, yet he must also be addressed and pointed to the sphere which lies beyond perception, the reality of which consists in man's relation to God.

20. Question 8 declares the universal sinfulness of man, with the reservation attaching to the regenerate Christian man. This reservation is not to be understood in the sense that the regenerate Christian man is plainly distinguishable, on the psychological level, from the natural man. It should be understood rather in the sense that sin is not reckoned as sin to the regenerate man who lives in the awareness of and under the inspiration of divine forgiveness. Thus man is transplanted to a state of life where, in a prefigurative way, he can act righteously.

21. Question 9 implies that the sinner sins through the bondage of his will, but is none the less responsible for his bondage. There exists a contradiction here only in speculative thought, which, by wrongly transferring the idea of freedom as the *liberum arbitrium*—valid in the moral and legal sphere—to the problematics of existence as a whole, seeks to escape the obligation to accept guilt. On the contrary, the very essence of existence is to be defined as integral responsibility.

22. True freedom, which is concerned with man's situation in regard to God and therefore with his existence as a whole, is the Augustinian conception of freedom for God. Sin really consists in the loss of this freedom. The loss of freedom corresponds to the fall of man, and so must be understood as transcendental, and as the condition underlying the possibility of all actual sinful thinking, speaking and doing which takes place in a state of bondage.

# CHAPTER 7

# GOD'S JUDGMENT AND WRATH

(Heidelberg Catechism, Questions 10 and 11)

Question 10. **"Will God allow such disobedience and apostasy to go unpunished? By no means: He is provoked to terrible anger both against inborn and actual sins, and wills by His just judgment to punish them in time and in eternity, as He has declared: 'Cursed be he who does not confirm the words of this law by doing them.' "**

Question 11. **"Is God then not merciful also? God is indeed merciful, but He is also just. Therefore His justice requires that sin, which is an offence against His supreme majesty, should be punished by extreme, that is, eternal, punishment striking both body and soul."**

### 1. *The Unity of Grace and Judgment*

THE DISCLOSURE of man's real situation must be taken further. So far we have been speaking about the guilt of man flowing from the non-fulfilment of the law, about "original sin", the enslavement of the will, and about the radical sinfulness of all mankind. This disclosure would not be complete if we did not go on to speak further of the judgment which guilt brings upon itself hence of man's misery arising from his sin. This theme, that of the misery which is the consequence of sin, should not however be misunderstood as implying, in terms of a causal sequence, a second and different factor following strictly upon the first. Judgment, the wretchedness of man, is not a new factor placed alongside sin. Rather, according to our pattern of thought, the explication of the one reality, it is an integral phase in one and the same situation, namely the unreality of man's being which hitherto we have met under the aspect of guilt.

And this one reality, the phenomenon of the falseness and

distortion of man's life, would not be sufficiently described if the aspect of judgment and hence of human misery were not expressly emphasized and considered in connexion with the aspect of guilt. As we have already said, in a certain sense, sin contains the judgment of God in itself. But this implication, the involvement of divine judgment in sin, must now be explained in its characteristic reality. Otherwise sin would not be understood as sin. Sin is sin through the judgment and condemnation of God. Without the development of this second aspect of the matter, the description of sin, remaining at the phenomenological stage, confined to the noting of the phenomenon itself, would be incomplete.

This inner consequence of sin is considered in Questions 10 and 11 of the Catechism, which declare the belief that man's sin "objectively" and in fact changes and disturbs his basic relation to God. Question 10 rejects the possibility for thought that the (as it were) "subjectively" sinful conduct of man, the sinful character of his existence, has no effect on his actual situation, and changes nothing as regards the reality of his life. "Will God allow such disobedience and apostasy to go unpunished? By no means!"

To what extent and *quo iure*, by what right, does this second aspect of judgment follow necessarily upon the first aspect of guilt? On what grounds do we know that God "will not allow such disobedience and apostasy to go unpunished", and that "He is provoked to terrible anger"? The sentence is an analytical one. We know of the wrath and judgment of God just because we are aware of sin as sin. Hence what is in question is not a "subjective" state of human existence which has no significance "objectively". This very distinction between the "subjective" and the "objective" aspects is impossible theologically; it would run counter to the idea of sin itself.[1] From the point of view of preaching, this state

---

[1] I here use the terms "objective" and "subjective" in inverted commas. The subject-object pattern of thought is overcome in theology through the religious consciousness of divine-human encounter. In the present instance, this is expressed in the fact that the "subjective" aspect of sin always contains implicitly an "objective" aspect—whence the distinction between the two aspects in the last resort loses all meaning.

of affairs means that we may never preach about sin as a merely subjective psychological condition deserving of judgment and punishment, but we must present it always and only as an actual disturbing of man's relation to God, as an impossible but in fact realized situation of mankind which already suffers the judgment of God, just because it deserves that judgment.

Question 11 concerns itself with an objection which from the fact of mercy as an attribute of God might infer the suspension of judgment as the "objective" consequence following upon guilt. The answer however insists on the actuality of judgment by referring to justice as another "attribute of God": "God is indeed merciful, but He is also just. Therefore His justice requires that sin, which is an offence against His supreme majesty, should be punished, by extreme, that is, eternal, punishment, striking both body and soul."

We cannot at this juncture examine closely the problems arising from the simple juxtaposition of two "attributes of God". In any case, the dialectic of the mercy and justice of God in Question 11 leads on to the second main part of the Catechism, which treats of man's redemption, and which shows how the mercy of the just God becomes effective for man and in the life of man. In any case, despite the problems involved in what we consider to be far too simple an argument, and therefore an unsatisfying one, we shall have to assent to the underlying intention and actual result of Question 11. For in the last analysis it is directed, like other questions which have preceded it, against an attempt to escape from the existential situation by speculative means. Guilt is indeed admitted, it is not disputed; yet man's responsibility is weakened and must finally cease, since no judgment follows upon guilt, because of course God, as we know, is merciful and in consequence will allow all such guiltiness to go unpunished. This is a speculative expedient inferred from the doctrine of God: the fact that the quality of mercy is to be ascribed to God is here used to extricate man from his true situation in which he is obliged to render account to God. It may be that this one example would inspire in us a general distrust of that type of theological discourse which treats of the "attributes of God". . . .

From the homiletic-kerygmatic point of view, Question 11 warns us against a too one-sided and doctrinaire proclamation of divine grace. Grace may not be preached about in terms of "cheap grace" (an expression which Bonhoeffer has rendered current). This means that it is not to be proclaimed as a mere theory about the God of grace, which in the last analysis cloaks human responsibility, which not only dissolves any sort of disquiet on the part of the sinner, but basically does not allow any such disquiet to emerge. Preaching of this type may lead to that particular doubt and self-torment which is sometimes met with, and which causes a man to say to himself that the grace of God is for all others except for himself. And this attitude occurs because he has not encountered the living and gracious God, but merely a theory of all-embracing divine grace.

How now are we to avoid a proclamation of cheap grace? Must we fall back on the scheme of the type of sermon in which the preaching of the gospel follows on the preaching of the law? Or shall we imperceptibly slide into a synergism which makes the reception of grace conditional upon man's co-operation (in order that in this way grace becomes not cheap but "dear")? There can of course be no question of adopting these solutions and it is not worth while to counter such types of thought with opposing arguments. No, the truth is that our preaching in the light of the warning implied in Question 11 acquires a different and a concrete feature, namely: grace must be preached about in such a way that it does not suspend or exclude the thought of divine judgment, but rather contains that thought in itself. The preaching of grace is implicitly the preaching of judgment. It is so, because it summons man to stand in the presence of God and therefore it summons him to responsibility. A true preaching of grace does not consist in an asseveration of the grace of God as though it were some neutral factor, some theory: it is a proclamation of the living God Himself, who is the ultimate reality for us, who is our God—even when He meets us as Judge.

This is the God who is concerned for us, who addresses to us His claim, who says: "I will be your God and ye shall be my people." Where this God is proclaimed, there is no need for an assertion of grace, and judgment is never excluded. There is no need to fling at the hearer a rigid "Thou shalt", for the proclamation will implicitly contain an appeal to him not to fail this God on any account. Thus we see that the preaching of a "cheap grace" has the character of an asseveration and a theory, whereas by contrast the proclamation of the living God implies, with grace, judgment also, with the result that the objection with which Question 11 is concerned to deal is from the outset impossible; the objection, namely, that a means of escape from divine judgment lies in the recourse to divine mercy. The dialectic of the judgment and mercy of God, which appears in Question 11, is therefore essentially the dialectic of judgment and grace. But this is not quite the same thing. What is questionable about Question 11 is that it transposes the dialectic of judgment and grace which is vitally necessary to all true preaching into the sphere of "divine attributes" and thus in fact it parries a metaphysical-speculative objection with a metaphysical-speculative answer.

## 2. *The Problem of the Personality of God*

To return to Question 10, which is still more important for our present argument: the instrument, the concept, by means of which the "trans-subjective" aspect of sin is maintained as governing the actual situation of human existence, is that of the "wrath of God". God is "provoked to terrible anger both against inborn and actual sins. . . ."

This idea of the divine wrath has been the cause of much vexation and offence. Thus the conception has been imputed to the Old Testament as something archaic, primitive and mythical, because it has been thought necessary to point out that it stands in contradiction to the New Testament revelation of divine love. This argument deserves little attention, for the simple reason that it rests upon an inattentive reading of both the Old and the New Testaments. To us the second criticism of the concept of the divine wrath seems much more important, namely the criticism which sees in it a piece of outmoded anthropomorphism which, in relation to God, the limit and the transcendence of our existence, appears unsuitable, unintelligible, and invalid. How is it possible to ascribe to God, who is quite plainly the limit and the ground of human life and of the whole order of creation, a human affection, a psychological datum?

This objection, this cause of offence, seems to us a serious one. In point of fact it has been quite early and quickly pointed out that the concept of the "wrath of God" means something quite other than an affection analogous to our human affections. What then do we mean by the wrath of God? Can we, and must we, hold fast to the idea? In accordance with our introductory point of view which again and again we have found to be a guide, a clue and a method, we put the question in dogmatic-homiletic terms: we pose the question of the kerygmatic and therefore the dogmatic legitimacy and necessity of the concept of the wrath of God. It might indeed seem as though the idea were superfluous, especially when we set out from the kerygmatic point of view. For how can we preach about the wrath of God? (In asking this last question, we must be clear about the fact that what is at issue here is not something peripheral and subordinate, not a possible theme of preaching, but rather the whole disclosure of the human situation inasmuch as the wrath of God—if acceptable—inheres in the proclamation of judgment as its inner ground; the latter, again, being integral to the proclamation of sin.)

In any case we preach the wrath of God—to proceed from the hypothesis of this point of view and this concept—not by delineating it in terms of human psychological behaviour. If it is to be understood, the preaching of it should rather seek to show the wrath of God as a factor overshadowing the given facts of human existence. In this sense the theme strikes man and enables him to understand his own concrete position in life as something which lies under the shadow of God's wrath and God's judgment. A typical expression of it is to be found in Psalm 90 which understands the transiency of man, and obviously not the transiency of earthly human life as such, but rather its qualified transiency—the perishability, the transitoriness, the nothingness of the passing moment, the failure to fill time with an enduring content—as an eminent manifestation of the wrath of God:

> For we are consumed by Thy anger; by Thy wrath we are overwhelmed. Thou hast set our iniquities before Thee, our secret sins in the light of Thy countenance. For all our days pass away under Thy wrath, our years come to an end like a sigh. . . . Who considers the power of Thy anger, and Thy wrath according to the fear of Thee?. . . . (vv. 7-9, 11).

From the last of the quoted verses we infer that the interpretation of human transitoriness here given is not something that is self-explanatory. The position is rather that a fact which is thoughtlessly regarded as self-explanatory, namely, the passing away of our days and years, is here referred to that its inner meaning may be illuminated, and explained from the point of view of the wrath of God and the judgment of God piercing to the heart of human existence. The fact that we exist to such an extent in nothingness and frailty, that we spend our years as though in idle chatter (more correctly, like a sigh—but Luther's translation shows such penetrating insight into the essence of the situation that in spite of the lexicon I prefer to adhere to it[1]) this fact, rightly considered, is by no means self-explanatory, it is rather monstrous and terrifying. The poet who wrote this psalm in prayerful thought recoils terrified before the abyss of human life, and recognizes in it the touch of the finger of God, that is, merited divine judgment. For existence in its nothingness is as terrifying as only the wrath of God can be terrifying. The horror-struck recoil in face of one's own nothingness—where it is existentially realized—is equivalent to terror in the face of God Himself. Whoever reaches this

---

[1] Reflections about the essential character of theological language might be made in connexion with such an example!

point in human existence suddenly becomes aware of standing under the judgment of God.

But if this is the case, if we can preach convincingly about the wrath of God only by showing the actual nothingness, the terrible frustrations of human life, what is the purpose of maintaining the symbolism of the wrath of God? Does it not become a superfluous and misunderstood mythological-anthropological vesture of what the preacher really has to say? Would not the purposes of preaching be better served if this anthropological outlook fell away and if such an abolition of outmoded anthropomorphism were sanctioned by dogmatics? Would it not be better if the preacher were allowed to limit himself, with a good conscience, to saying what is really to be said and demonstrated, convincingly and intelligibly, about the realities of human life itself, namely the nothingness, the vanity, the frustration, in which man exists in the face of God?

But if we did this, the fact of human nothingness and vanity would not become something independently given. Even then sin would remain as sin against God. The relationship to God, to the *extra nos* (outside ourselves) would remain intact: for the unreality and falsity of human life, defined from our point of departure, is a matter of being apart from God. And this being apart from, in separation from, God, bears within itself the judgment: but that and nothing else is clearly what we mean by the wrath of God. . . .

Over and above this, which is what is obviously meant in this connexion, what meaning can be attached, existentially, to specific talk about a divine wrath? If it could be shown that no existential relevance attached to this theological concept, then, in accordance with our scheme, dogmatics would have to be revised at this point, for basically dogmatics may contain nothing other than what in preaching may be a truth whereby man is challenged and addressed.

Nevertheless on the other hand the question must here be asked: is it sufficient, do we, from a purely existential point of view, remain adequate to the expression of the intended truth, to the explication of the one reality and of

our factual situation, when we talk merely about the unreality and falsity of human life—even though the latter is
understood as unreality in the sight of God? Does not rather
the 90th Psalm express the point more adequately in that
it refers us to the wrath of God Himself? The conception of
a human unreality, a distortion of human life which is not
accompanied, or rather constituted, by the wrath of God
Himself, which in a certain sense leaves God unaffected,
would probably reflect Schleiermacher's idea of sin as
something which is operative in a merely subjective sense,
in a manward way (objective of course in so far as it changes
man's actual relation to God) but which leaves God Himself
unaffected. God Himself stands completely "outside the
situation": the sin of man can in no wise concern Him.

At this juncture we might refer to Bultmann, who,
although he nowhere explicitly expresses his mind on the
matter, must probably be seen as coinciding with the thought
of Schleiermacher (by the impulsion of his own presupposi-
tions); for to him the sting of sin lies in any case in the sphere
of self-understanding, whilst "God Himself", "God in person" represents a point of view which transcends this horizon
and so for Bultmann can hardly come into consideration.
And one might be inclined to give scope to this view of things,
precisely because Bultmann's whole theological thinking
has an eminently kerygmatic orientation and because in
particular his leading idea of self-understanding is intended
to emphasize the character of preaching as a personal address.

But it is just this point of view of Bultmann and his
presumable attitude in this matter which points us to the
issue which is really at stake in this problem of the wrath of
God: here there emerges and conspicuously so, for the first
time, within the horizon of this question about the disclosure
of man's true situation, the personality of God and the personal character of the relationship between man and God.
It is this point that is really at stake. No doubt the unreality
and falsity of human life (as a manifestation of the "divine
wrath") is in a certain sense demonstrable, whereas the
wrath of God itself lies obviously beyond human perception.

Nevertheless, if the relationship within which the unreality of human life is to be seen primarily as reflecting the judgment of God, is to be maintained in its personal character, and to be shown as a personal confrontation, then the idea of the divine wrath becomes unavoidable. Without this concept it would be possible perhaps to speak of a personal God, but the personality of God would not be confirmed at the vital point (*quoad nos*, where we are concerned) namely that of the divine-human encounter. An encounter with God in which we experience our unreality as divine judgment, but which leaves God Himself unaffected, would be a relationship of which the personal note itself was impaired.

I am of course well aware of the problematics which surround the whole conception of the personality of God. How far we should speak of personality or supra-personality (certainly not of impersonality or sub-personality!) in reference to God, is a question which should be treated under the heading of the doctrine of the Trinity. For ourselves this basic question does not here come under discussion. Nor will its decision change in any way the *desideratum* which we have just intimated: the encounter with God from which all preaching flows and to which it points and towards which dogmatics also must be orientated, is in any event a personal encounter. And the idea of the wrath of God as a theologoumenon is a dogmatic correlate, a dogmatic expression of the personal character of that encounter. The divine-human encounter is personal, because it includes decision, responsibility and guilt. But we can only speak of decision, responsibility and guilt when we are in the fullest sense confronted by a person, a self that is capable of love and anger, which means, however, capable on his side too of decision and responsibility.

This last train of thought may seem somewhat offensive and bewildering. Are we not in fact applying a general principle (for example the principle of a personalistic, philosophically ethical world-view) by means of which we then infer as by a syllogism the personality of God from the character of our own life? But can the personality of God be inferred? I maintain however that

—contrary to the *prima facie* view—there is not to be found here a conclusion in the sense of classical deduction, in the syllogistic sense. For we must make it clear to ourselves that the categories or the existential features of personal being are not at our disposal. They elude our control. We first gain some intimation of them in the illumination of our own being through its encounters and experiences, also—and especially—through the illumination which results from our encounter with God. For this reason the concept of "personality" in general cannot function as a premiss, from which the personality of God is then concluded. It is rather that encounter with God, the deep-rooted faith-situation of our life is the more original factor, in the light of which there springs to view the quality of personality (that of our own existence as well as that of the existence of God). Thus our argument through the existential factor of personality does not rest on a process of deduction, but is rather an explication of the situation of faith. (This is also shown in the fact that the structure of personality which we have used is by no means fully worked out by us.)

It might seem further offensive and bewildering that we have spoken of decision and responsibility in relation to the being of God Himself (in virtue of His personality). But here again we are not simply presupposing unproved views, nor are we drawing *in abstracto* a conclusion by analogy. It is rather that here again we are simply describing and illuminating a situation (and I would claim that this approach is the plain theological method). We are only using the concepts of decision and responsibility in this connexion in order to grapple, as closely as possible, with the phenomenon which is in question, namely that of our own faith-situation in the sight of God. We claim that this situation of ours is a personal one and we are using the two concepts referred to in order to make a tentative description of what we mean thereby.

We experience and understand (in a very primary and immediate way, hence in the sense of original "self-understanding") our relationship to God through faith as something which is analogous to our relationship to our fellow men, that is, to persons and as being also essentially distinct from our relationship to things: hence it is in its essence a personal relationship. We are not proposing however to make the analysis of our relationship to human persons into a norm for our relationship to God. It is clear to us from the outset that in man's relation to God a conception of personality *sui generis*, in a class by itself, must come into play. In contradistinction to particular human relationships, there is here involved a personal mode of relationship which has an utterly all-embracing universal character, inasmuch as it unconditionally concerns the human person who is engaged, it affects him wholly in all the dimensions of his life and therefore it claims him in an utterly other, total, way.

And we must note well that this implies a difference not of quantity only, but of quality, in the structure of the relationship. The total nature of the relationship fundamentally changes the structure itself. (From this point of view we might inquire into the structural connexion between the divine-human relationship and the inter-human relationship. Might it not be that this latter is determined in its essence by the former, and that apart from encounter with God we can attain no ultimate existential insight into the basic character of the inter-human personal relationship?) In any case the somewhat clumsy analogy between man's relation with God and his relation with his fellow men (as distinct from his relation with things), and assuming the reservation we have indicated, does make possible a certain preliminary insight into the essence of man's relationship with God as something distinctively personal.

Undoubtedly we speak also about personal communion with spiritual worlds and values and such like—and we mean thereby a personal encounter in a very special sense. Hence it is here a question not of communion with a person, but of communion with a neutral, a "content", an atmosphere. (We might think for example of what is implied in intellectual and spiritual communion with the world of antiquity.) None the less even such a type of communion, where it really strikes a man, will have as its consequence decisions and thus responsibilities. It will do so, in fact, when it produces its effects in the sphere of personal relations, and thus proves itself to have had the character of genuine spiritual communion. Here again therefore the personal aspect comes into play. (Whether and to what an extent it is also possible to speak of communion with nature, with an animal for example, a plant or a landscape, would be a point needing special clarification. A landscape, in so far as it truly becomes the subject of a special communion and inspiration—and this is indeed possible—seems to me to be somewhat like a "spiritual" world or a world of ideas.) Hence encounter with the neutral factor of a "world" appears as something "derivative", or perhaps it would be better to say that it is a "preparatory encounter", which reaches its consummation only in personal encounter in the fullest sense.

But the encounter with God cannot possibly be described as being preparatory to personal fellowship among men. It is rather the highest term, a plenitude, which integrates into itself the reality of all other encounters, all other forms of communion, so that in a sense inter-human personal relationships (analogously to the train of thought which has just been expressed) may be claimed as preparatory to the supreme encounter with God. Man's relation to God is therefore, to be sure, no relation with an "it", but a "thou" relation, or indeed more, a "thou" relationship in a super-eminent and ultimate sense.

Hence we are not using the concept of the personality of God as our point of departure, for by doing so we should be simply passing over still unclarified problems. We take rather as our point of departure the personal character of man's encounter with God. Encounter as such, the situation in which faith is rooted, the situation which we are clarifying in theological thinking, has a basically personal character. And such personal character implies decision, guilt, and responsibility on our side. So much springs from the clarification of our own human situation.

But at the same time—since it is just not a question of encounter with an "it"—there must also be presupposed something in the nature of decision and responsibility on the "other side". Otherwise the personal nature of our own situation would become emptied of real meaning; our talk of it would cease to be meaningful. In other words, the concepts of responsibility and decision imply, or rather demand, that there should be responsibility and decision on the "other side" also, in the Person with whom we are confronted.

They demand and imply that One stands over against us who is capable of decision and responsibility (the ideas of "decision" and "responsibility" are indissolubly inter-connected—a point which remains to be further investigated), that is, they utterly demand and imply personality. Otherwise, from a purely phenomenological point of view, there would be no sense at all in talking about decision and responsibility. These concepts are by their very nature rooted in the climate of personality. The animal can neither decide nor accept responsibility. But the personal horizon implies also—again by its very nature—a confrontation of the "I" and "thou". Hence the concepts "decision" and "responsibility" are once again evacuated of their true content once they are cut loose from the experience of confrontation between the "I" and the "thou". Even decisions in relation to a world of ideas, an "it", as we have already seen, prepare the way for personal encounters and decisions.

We deduce from all this (again by way of phenomenological description and explication) that when we think that we are correctly and appropriately describing our own faith-situation by using such concepts as "decision" and "responsibility", we are in fact implicitly presupposing also the personality of God or at least the personal nature of man's relation to God (and thus at the very least the "personal character" of the One who "stands over against us"). We have presupposed that God on His side too makes decisions and stands guarantor of those decisions. Of course this again is no simple analogical and therefore anthropomorphic transference of the two concepts or "qualities" to the being of God. It is an inescapable conclusion flowing from the real, factual character which marks the confrontation of man by God, and from the specific structure of meaning which that actual experience contains.

It is of the first importance to be clear that our present argument rests on a wholly different basis from that of the argument by analogy. When by analogy we transfer to the being of God (on the basis of an always presupposed fundamental analogy: the *analogia entis*) certain human and creaturely qualities which we think we recognize in the realm of creation, then the concepts of the qualities concerned become for us governing concepts which may be predicated both of the creature and also (perhaps in a somewhat modified sense) of the Creator. The thinker who makes such a transference of ideas from created being to the being of the Creator is in a sense claiming to stand at a vantage-point from which he can hold in his perspective both the creation and its Creator: for he is able to conceive of the governing idea which embraces both. But the thinker who, from within the personal nature of his own existential situation, becomes aware of the personality of the One by whom he is confronted, and proceeds to explicate what he is ever intuitively aware of because of his personal involvement in the situation, such a one remains strictly within the situation and renounces any attempt to reach a speculative point of view which would enable him to transcend it. His sequence of thought is an immanent clarification of the situation from within and nothing further. It is a question of nothing other than an understanding of the existential situation flowing from the heart of that situation: and it is just this kind of theology which may be described as the "movement and inspiration of faith".

In this matter of the problem of the personality of God, there can at most be a quite external and formal affinity between an illumination of the situation from within the experience of it—which is what we are striving to attain— and an analogical-speculative theory about the being of God. I attach the greatest importance to making clear these methodological differences of approach to the question, because at this momentous juncture of our argument, where for the first time in our theological inquiry the right understanding of the personality of God is at stake, we must not render ourselves open to the reproach of disingenuousness or slovenliness of method.

The structural interconnexion of the concepts "decision", "responsibility" and "personality" is no doubt a matter which we have as yet insufficiently clarified. We must resign the attempt to make any such deeper investigation in this discussion and accept the interconnexion, in preliminary fashion, as something given. It is in a sense something self-evident. None the less we remain fully aware of the wider task which here awaits the thinker, and, in renouncing it, consider that we are not guilty of any unmethodical curtailment of the scope of the problem.

Now, in harmony with our own immediate experience of the faith-situation in which our human personality is engaged, and which we have recognized as being characterized by the notes of decision and responsibility, we have spoken of the decision and responsibility *of God*. Such ideas however now assume a different nuance, in fact, in some sense, a different meaning: for God's decisions have not the character of risk and daring which marks all human decisions. God's decisions are His eternal counsels. But it is just in the fulfilment of these His eternal counsels that God stands over against us in confrontation. By means of them, as it were, He delimits the horizons within which all our own decisions become possible. Again we must speak of God's responsibility, but in a somewhat modified sense. Such language applied to God does not mean that He owes something to some one or that He is answerable to human beings for His decisions. (It is in this latter sense that we must understand our own human responsibility, which is our obligation to render account to God as our Judge.) God's responsibility consists in His fidelity. It means that He remains ever faithful to His eternal counsels, that He "stands by" His decisions. It is as this ever faithful God that He meets us.

God's own faithfulness marks out the horizon within which our own responsibility comes into play. His faithfulness is the "salvation-bringing *a priori*" (the basic condition of possibility) underlying the emergence of our own responsibility, just as His eternal counsels are the "salvation-bringing *a priori*" underlying the possibility of our own decisions. By His constancy and fidelity, by the fact that He is the same, yesterday, today and for ever, God challenges us to radical, limitless and continuing responsibility. He brings us thus into confrontation with Himself, and demands that we be constant in conformity with His own constancy. Only through the constancy and the continuity of a consistently, perseveringly, responsible life could we be conformed to the abiding fidelity of God. And such conformity He rightly requires of us, in that He has willed, wills and shall ever will to be our God, in that He meets us as God the ever-faithful.

But it is just the challenge of this demand that we fail

to meet. Our own responsibility before God remains but fitfully fulfilled or else is not fulfilled at all. . . . We live as though God were not. But even though we fail to fulfil the divine demand, and thus utterly fail in loyalty to God Himself, we cannot escape the requirement of responsibility, and in the end it will overtake us and finally confront us with its authority at the Judgment Day. In the idea of responsibility there is always implicit the note of constancy and faithfulness: inasmuch as I accept responsibility for my being and doing, I preserve my own continuity of life, I remain true to myself as a person, I remain constant as the person that I am. I stand indissolubly linked to what I have been and what I have done.

Such continuity in responsible personal being might be regarded as something voluptuous to be enjoyed, as a possibility of being to be either arbitrarily adopted or arbitrarily rejected, and alongside it we might consider as equally valid the possibility of an ever-shifting flux of personality—were it not for the ultimate reality of God, were it not for the fact that He is the Immanuel, God with us. . . . But God is, He confronts me as the One who is eternally faithful to Himself, and who is therefore also eternally faithful to me. Hence by right I have no choice, there is for me only the one possibility of life, that of responsible faithfulness—and any alternative possibility of life I could choose only *per nefas*, prompted by evil. Responsibility, and the obligation to accept life in responsibility, has become inescapable, ineluctable. I can by right exist before God only as responsible man. This implies however at the same time the possibility of sin and failure and disloyalty. The constancy of God demands my constancy. His faithfulness is the ground of my existence in responsibility.

### 3. *The God of Love and Wrath*

As we have predicated personality, together with its essential aspects of decision and responsibility, as something inherent in our experience of God—and this not by means of any analogical-speculative method of transference but by an existential illumination of an existential situation—so now and consistently with that point of view, we have to establish love and anger as irreducible moments in personality. And this again we shall do, not as an affirmation about the divine being in itself, but as a function of that personal encounter in which we find ourselves placed. The structural interconnexion between decision and responsibility on the one hand, and love and anger on the other, would have to be shown by a deeper analysis. I content myself at this juncture with indicating the problem:

Could responsibility and genuine decision be possible in confrontation with a being which knows neither love nor wrath? In such a case, in fact, could there be any meaning in talking about personal confrontation? When we refer to love and anger we are not of course thinking of feelings of sympathy and antipathy as psychological data. So far as we can observe love and anger at work in the human sphere of life, they are values which are constantly given as an inextricable part of the situation. But were we to develop our understanding of divine love and anger from this point of view, that is, in psychological terms, it would be altogether too superficial. We should not reach an essential understanding of the matter on these lines. Here it again becomes clear that the existential analysis surpasses the psychological one, without rendering the latter useless. Psychology notes phenomena correctly and helps towards an understanding of life, but it does not penetrate to the underlying essence. Only when psychology transforms its own mode of approach to things into an absolute value, only when it becomes psychologism, is it false!

In the present instance therefore it is a question of describing existentially the phenomena of love and anger and thus penetrating more deeply than the psychological insights, which are correct in themselves. If we do this we reach the conclusion (which I anticipate here as a presumption without carrying out the tedious analysis that would be necessary to prove it) that a being which knows neither love nor anger is a being which does not engage itself. As such—from the point of view of personal decision and responsibility—it would not give rise to genuine confrontation. How could genuine decision and responsibility be at all possible in confrontation with a being which knows nothing of personal commitment, personal engagement? The concepts of decision and responsibility as intimating the basic existential features of the personal situation of man require that the One who stands over against him should be engaged. For it is in decision and responsibility that man engages himself. And such self-engagement is possible only if we stand over against a being who on his side too enters into engagement.

In this context we might amplify the word which we have chosen, the word "engagement", by saying that it implies pledging one's self, staking one's life on a certain issue. And the ideas of love and anger connote such a self-commitment, such a pledging of oneself. One cannot love provisionally or for the time being, as one can play chess for the time being. (For this reason one can play chess even against an automatic antagonist!) It is in this sense of engagement and self-commitment that we should prefer to speak of the love and also of the anger of God—not in the sense, not according to the analogy, of human affections which it is possible to study only in the sphere of earthly realities open to our perception.

In conclusion I would formulate the matter as follows: to deny love and anger in God would be equivalent to rejecting the notion of personality in God. This however would mean nothing other than excluding from faith its personal overtones, denying it its character of decision and responsibility. At best there would then remain only the possibility of characterizing faith as consisting of subjective emotions.

To sum up: a long and somewhat complicated train of thought, starting from the question of the homiletic and dogmatic legitimacy of the concept of the divine wrath, caused us to circle round the problem of the personality of God in general. The much disputed doctrine of the wrath of God (which is in the truest sense worthy of being questioned) brings forward for the first time, in the context of our inquiry into man's real situation in the eyes of God, the whole problem of personality in God and lends it urgency and actuality.

Various existential analyses were made as ramifications of this main theme. In this connexion some problems were deliberately outlined only and the solution briefly indicated by way of anticipation. Perhaps despite the arid conceptual character of our train of reasoning, the enthusiasm behind our thinking and the feeling for breadth may have given some intimation of how much is still to be thought and understood on these themes . . .

In all our arguments about the personality of God, we were greatly concerned, from a methodological point of view, to dispel the false appearance of a speculative mode of thought such as transfers by analogy to the being of God the features which are seen to characterize human personality. We have been anxious to show, on the contrary, that it can only be a question here of illuminating, in a genuinely theological manner, that is, by phenomenological description, by existential explication, the self-understanding of that existential situation in which, when we live by faith, we always find ourselves placed. The self-understanding of faith is a personal factor, the situation itself is personal. And from that point of view it is not "concluded" that God is personal, but rather the statement we make on the basis of self-understanding implies the notion of personality in God, for all personal and genuine decision and responsibility demands of necessity that the Other by whom it is confronted and challenged should be personal and personally engaged.

In so far as I understand my faith not only as assent, or as subjective emotion, but as life in decision and responsibility (which means life in personal terms) I must always reckon with God as personal: in this situation God has always become for me the "thou" by whom I stand confronted. And it must be understood that this is not primarily a theological notion, it is the wholly original, existential self-understanding of the life of faith. Faith, seen as existence in decision and responsibility, contains implicitly the "thou" of the Other who stands over against it. Hence it implies personality in God, and apart from this it is unthinkable. This is of course no demonstration of the existence of God; it is not an argument leading to the conclusion that this "thou", this Other by whom it is confronted, must exist. But it is a basic feature of the self-understanding of religious faith; unless it is respected, the phenomenon of faith cannot be understood at all, cannot be appraised, cannot be clearly appreciated and assessed in that which it wills to be.

The ideas of decision and responsibility as the *propria*, the distinguishing marks, of the personal are derived, in the first place, from the clarification of personal encounter between human beings with all that it implies. Nevertheless, as we have seen, two qualifications must be noted: firstly, in the sphere of human experience, there are also encounters, deserving of the name, which are not strictly personal encounters but apprehensions of an "it", for example of a whole world of ideas. Secondly, we cannot conceive quite simply of what is involved in the personal nature of encounter with God on the analogy of the personal element in the sphere of inter-human relationships. For here there emerges an aspect of totality which changes the whole structure.

We then came to a recognition of the difference between human decisions and the divine counsels, between human responsibility and divine faithfulness. At the same time it became clear that the divine plan is the *a priori* basis for human decisions, just as the divine faithfulness is the *a priori* foundation on which human responsibility is constituted.

We next reached the conclusion that the experience of the "it" was a "preparatory" stage leading to the human encounter with the "thou", while the latter (or rather both) could be understood as preparatory to the divine-human encounter, since the experience of confrontation by God is the plenitude, the consummation, the integration of all human experience of encounter and personal communion.

This gradation in man's experience of personal encounter belongs however to problems which must be left open for further investigation. Perhaps at first glance it may seem evident and striking that this view has affinities with the gradations of being which are established in the scholastic picture of the world and idea of God. None the less it is quite plain that the latter outlook is based on an unambiguous ontology which is very different from our own.

Among the problems we have left open belongs further that of the structural interconnexion between personality, decision and responsibility (and consequently the question of a precise definition of these concepts). Further there is the problem of the interconnexion between the pairs of ideas: decision and responsibility on the one hand, love and anger on the other. In this respect, some light may well be thrown on the problem by an examination of the frequent Old Testament expression "*hesed wa'emeth*", i.e. "grace and truth" or "mercy and faithfulness". Love and faithfulness (cf. above: faithfulness and responsibility) are clearly linked by an inner, indissoluble connexion. Thus the two pairs of ideas meet and the meeting point of all these ideas lies in the rightly understood idea of personality. In a preliminary way we defined love (and so also its correlate: anger) in formal terms as engagement, self-commitment. And on both sides this engagement again is implicit in the self-understanding both of inter-human personal relations and of man's relation to God in faith. Faith's understanding of itself as a matter of decision and responsibility always presupposes that God can love and be wrathful. It presupposes that man's relation to God is fraught with ultimate seriousness, that is to say, that God pledges Himself in this situation, that for Him it is a matter of ultimate concern in which He involves Himself.

A further step is to be taken here: is not the aspect of divine self-engagement (which we have seen to be necessary) in the divine-human encounter sufficiently preserved when we speak only of the love of God? Must we go further and speak in addition of the wrath of God? In any event, love and wrath are correlative. He who cannot really love cannot really be angry either—and the converse. The same is true of anger which we have already declared to be true of love: one cannot be angry incidentally and casually as one might be playing chess incidentally. Neither can one really be angry with a thing or an animal, only with a person. Anger presupposes the same kind of self-commitment and concern as love. We might however be angry with God—basically— except that we have no right to be so (and no basis for such an attitude). Nor in the last analysis have we any right to be angry with our neighbour, our brother. God alone has a right to anger, because He alone is perfectly faithful.

Moreover this idea of anger towards God is surrounded with exactly the same series of problems as is that of man's love towards God. What is the meaning of "loving God"? "No one has seen God at any time" . . . (The best that I know on this point occurs in Karl Barth: "Love of God spells the deepest reality in face of the whole problem of our life!" *Römerbrief*, p. 302.)[1] Love and anger are inextricably related to each other and condition each other. Were we to speak only of the love of God, disregarding the idea of His wrath, then the freedom of God would be surrendered: God would no longer be "the One Who loves in freedom" (Karl Barth). The divine love would have become a necessary, and, as it were, automatic, mechanically released expression of His being. This amounts to saying that love would no longer be truly love: that that all-integrating structural aspect in the personal character of the divine-human encounter would have been surrendered. From this angle too the concept of the wrath of God proves itself to be, in particular, a notable test of the personal understanding of faith.

Barth moreover showed most impressively the interconnexion between the love and anger of God in his commentary on the Heidelberg Catechism, when, considering Question 11 ("God is indeed merciful, but He is also just") he expressed himself in the following way:

"God is merciful inasmuch as He is just. When God's right is

---

[1] E.T. *The Epistle to the Romans*, 1933.

violated, then also man's right is at an end. So close and intimate is the relation between God and man. If God does not wish to leave man's own right in ruins, then also His own divine right must be restored. The honour of God and also man's salvation depend on this—that the destruction of order is intolerable, and that therefore the forgiveness of sins cannot mean an overlooking of wrong. The destruction of order must be seen to be such and as such be wiped out. 'The wrath of God is terrible . . .'

"In the Christian Church and in theology there has been much perplexity at times about this idea of the wrath of God, and religious men have been distressed and vexed by it. And it has then been proposed that at this point scripture ought to be improved, since the conception of God's anger is unworthy. In particular Albert Ritschl attempted to eliminate the idea by clever, sophisticated exegesis. This however is an impossible undertaking and contradicts the whole meaning of the Gospel. For when Holy Scripture and, following it, the Heidelberg Catechism speak about the wrath of God, they intend to point to the fact that God is the living God, that He is near to man, that He is concerned about man, in fact so near and so concerned, that it is possible for man to injure His 'supreme majesty'. By entering with man into a covenant of grace, God has drawn so near to man that He can be affected, wounded, by what man is and does. The being and the doing of man pierce the heart of God. . . . A mere condoning pardon would neither be worthy of God, nor would it be salutary to man. It would be tantamount to the unmercifulness and indifference of a God who would not be truly God" (*op. cit.* pp. 36ff.).

Barth's talk about the "right of God" and the "right of man" which are closely interdependent and both of which must be restored, sounds extremely legalistic and so objectivizing from the point of view of existential thought; but it is not so in reality. It is of the highest existential relevance, a relevance which deserves to be coherently explained and elucidated. In his defence of the idea of the wrath of God, Barth proposes to say nothing other than that God takes man seriously, in that He pledges Himself to, involves Himself in the relationship with man which He Himself has set up. And this means that the divine wrath is an aspect of the overflowing, all-embracing mercy of God; a mercy which leads God in such a way to take man up into an unsurpassable fellowship with Himself, and with ultimate seriousness to enter into this partnership with man.

The wrath of God confirms the mercy of God. Apart from divine wrath, the relationship of man with God would not be serious and final; faith would become an illusion. God would no longer be God—He would cease to exist for us if the relationship in which He confronts man were to be emptied of meaning and content.

In order to illustrate our argument, let us, for instance, consider the point of view of pantheism (and all talk of a loving God who knows not anger and so is deprived of freedom would have to be described, in the last resort, as pantheistic[1]): for pantheism there may well be the experience of responsibility, but only as a phenomenon on a secondary, purely immanentist, inter-human plane. The pantheist knows the meaning of human faithfulness. He may too develop an ethic by making an appeal to the ultimate ground of being as the theoretical basis and support for the moral life. But only in theory. For there cannot be on this view an experience of responsibility in face of the Absolute and Ultimate itself. Hence the attempt to base human responsibility on the ultimate ground of being remains a theoretical, ideological buttressing of it, and, in the last analysis, no more than a phrase. (This however does not mean that man's responsibility before God, if really faced and accepted by the pantheist, has no value in the sight of God.) But responsibility over against the God understood as God by the pantheist is and remains no more than sounding brass or clanging cymbal!

After this prolonged excursus on the ontology rooted in the concept of personality, we now return to a question of homiletics: namely, whether and to what extent a development of the theme of God's wrath is justified and necessary in preaching?

Our discussion has shown us that from the standpoint of the self-understanding of faith there can be no question of relinquishing this theme. It seems to us that Psalm 90 deals with the theme in the most appropriate and acceptable and convincing manner when on the one hand it discloses

[1] We are here using the term pantheism in a broad sense: it includes, for example, that outlook which has sometimes been called deistic.

the judgment of God working out its effects in the existential sphere of man's sheer experience of life, and on the other hand does not hesitate to describe the factor underlying the vicissitudes of human life as the wrath of God. Thus man's encounters with the "it" and the "thou", and in fact the whole of his experience of life, are integrated in this ultimate encounter with the "Thou" who is the source of his being. All that is existentially real to man receives its ultimate qualification from this supreme communion with Personality. For our part we shall attempt to preach in this way, so long as we wish to confront the hearer with the reality of the living God and to summon him to responsibility before this God. In regard to the wrath of God, we do not need to be more specific and concrete. We may not be so, if we do not wish to deteriorate into psychological speculations. We are sufficiently concrete and in fact could not be more so, if, following Psalm 90, we connect our discourse with the changes and chances of life itself. For it is in the ever-changing phenomena of human existence that the wrath of God becomes concretely manifest. But the emphatic declaration: "Such is the power of *Thy wrath*, that we pass away thus, and of *Thy anger* that we so suddenly are cast into the abyss . . ." is by no means superfluous!

### 4. *"Inborn" and "Actual" Sins*

There still remain two parts of the 10th Question and Answer which need elucidation: namely, that God "is provoked to terrible anger both against inborn and actual sins. . . ." and that "He wills by His just judgment to punish them in time and in eternity." What is the meaning of this twofold duality —i.e. inborn and actual sins and punishment both in time and in eternity?

In the Catechism the purpose of the distinction between inborn and actual sins and their specific mention is to avoid any suggestion that one of these two types of sin, namely "inborn sin", is exempt from the wrathful judgment of God, on the ground that there, although indeed it is a question of sin, man "cannot help it". God is not unjust, when He punishes man even for his "inborn sin". In this way, the integral judgment of God and the integral responsibility of man is firmly maintained. Thus far, the doctrine corresponds absolutely with the understanding of sin which we have hitherto developed. Nevertheless, in the light of our transcendental interpretation of the fall and original sin, we can no longer speak in the same way of "inborn", that is, inherited sin. In this regard, we prefer to speak of our sinful disposition and inclinations, which are linked to, and perhaps in fact decisively determined by, the fact that we live in a sinful world and society. "Woe is me! For I am lost; for I am a man of unclean lips, and I dwell in the midst of a people of unclean lips" (Isa. 6:5).

That God "is provoked to terrible anger" by such solidarity in sin means that He reckons to my account the guilt of society, that He addresses me as one who is guilty through my incorporation in a guilty society. It certainly does not mean that His wrath is directed against me both on account of the sins for which I am responsible and also on account of the sins for which I am not responsible. Rather it is that responsibility is something integral and all-inclusive. And the allusion (so easily misunderstood) to "inborn sin", as also the allusion to "unrecognized sin" in Psalm 90, may legitimately become the theme of a preaching which proposes to appeal to man to give up his moralistic understanding of sin as consisting only in *peccatum actuale* in favour of such an integral, comprehensive, acceptance of responsibility for corporate guilt. The point that is being expressed in this summons is as follows: when I really have to do with the living God, it is no longer permitted to me, it is no longer possible for me to lay before God, as it were, that amount of sin for which I deem myself responsible; in other words to delimit, in the face of God, the proportion of my personal responsibility. When I have to do with the living God Himself, then what is demanded of me is the unlimited readiness to accept total responsibility.

I am aware that in this situation I am wholly surrendered to the judgment of God, who knows me better than I know myself. I must therefore be ready to shoulder also the responsibility of things which I am not yet conscious of being responsible for. Because God is God, I have from the start to sign a blank cheque for the admission of my guilt (and this action that is required of me is, let it be well understood, no *sacrificium intellectus!*). For the fact is that God is no human partner. Faced by a human partner there can be limits assigned to the acceptance of responsibility. I myself can become clearly aware of these limits, and can perhaps invoke them when I declare that in certain areas of my life I am determined to be answerable not before men but before God alone. No one can rightly hinder me in this, for every servant stands or falls to his own master (Rom. 14:4). The inner core of personal being, the ultimate essence of personality, lies in the region of personal life where man is alone before God, where he knows that he is responsible to God alone. In this, his neighbour is not cheated of his due, for our responsibility towards him is in any event from the very outset not an integral one. On the contrary, it is salutary as regards our relation to our neighbour that certain things, although they are indeed to be answered for, yet can be decided not before him, but before some other bar of judgment. But where man sees himself to be set over against God Himself, then no escape and no delimitation is possible.

Something of this understanding of total responsibility flashes forth and is made convincing in an impressively poetical way in one of the greatest novels of our century, namely in Franz Kafka's *Prozess*,[1] in which a man who is conscious of no essential sin is nevertheless accused and condemned to death, and at the end bows before the justice of the judgment. Our preaching about sin and judgment must not fall short of this penetrating insight into the basic realities of human life!

What is also striking in Question 10 is that no difference of degree is established between "inborn" and "actual" sins. It is not suggested for example that *peccatum actuale* weighs more heavily with God, and is more strictly punished by

---

[1] E.T. *The Trial*, new edn. 1956.

Him, than is the sinful disposition. The conception of total responsibility does not permit of such gradations. It includes in one *totum* both inborn and actual sins, in such a way that "inborn sin", or the transcendental primal guilt which discloses and confirms its prior existence in every actual sin, utterly surpasses these and is of more gravity than the sum total of all the actual sins that man commits.

### 5. *Temporal and Eternal Punishment*

Finally, as far as the distinction between temporal and eternal punishment is concerned, the relation between the two must be understood on similar lines to our understanding of the distinction between inborn and actual sin: eternal punishment is manifested in temporal punishment, just as inborn sin manifests itself in actual sin.

This distinction forms an aspect in the believer's understanding of his own religious consciousness. What is expressed in speaking of eternal punishment is that, in the encounter between guilty man and the God of judgment, what is at issue is "that which unconditionally concerns us"; in other words the eternal destiny of man. This point can be effectively expressed only if we speak of eternal punishment; and only through the concept of eternal punishment can we effectually make it understood that the relation between man and God is really and radically disturbed. In speaking of temporal punishment on the other hand we are expressing the fact that such divine judgment is no abstraction, indifferent to the way in which man lives in the course of his earthly life, but that man is warned not needlessly to accept concretely experienced events and features in his life as so much mere chance, but rather to see them as the working out of the judgment of God, and in planning the actions of his earthly life seriously, to fear the impact of such temporal punishment in the future. The transience, frailty and frustrations of human life as depicted in Psalm 90 form an example of temporal punishment.

None the less, temporal and eternal punishment are not distinct, co-ordinated punitive measures taken by God.

Punishment forms an indissoluble whole as sin forms an indissoluble whole: the desire to live apart from God is overtaken by the punishment of having to live apart from God. Hence the relation between punishment in time and punishment in eternity is not that of a juxtaposition, but of an interweaving into one texture of reality: in temporal punishment eternal punishment foreshadows itself or rather already manifests itself. . . .

Hence the preacher must not recoil from speaking of divine punishment in concrete and vivid terms. But this must not be done in a series of mere assertions, by affirming of this or that event that it must be understood as a punishment sent by God, but rather, once more, by way of exposing man's true situation. He must try convincingly to show that certain eventualities and features of human existence are manifestations of eternal punishment in the sense of fundamental separation from God, and hence must be understood as temporal punishment. He cannot of course do this by formulating general principles, by asserting that this or that must at all events be understood as indicating the temporal punishment sent by God. . . . He can only do so by appealing to his hearer to engage in a distinct act of self-examination and self-understanding *hic et nunc*.

If then eternal punishment (which cannot be formulated in human affirmations, but which rather formulates itself, proleptically, in the experiences which strike us in the course of our earthly lives) announces and manifests itself in temporal punishment, a further differentiation between the two things can and must be made on the basis of the confession of Christian faith in Question 1 of the Catechism.

While through our faith in Jesus Christ we understand that eternal punishment, the final and absolute separation from God, has been annulled for us as believers, nevertheless temporal punishments, as manifestations of this ultimate menace which has now been dispelled for us, still remain. Now "in all affliction and persecution with raised head I await the Judge who has already appeared on my behalf before the judgment of God, and has removed from me the threat of becoming accursed. . . ." (Question 52). Temporal punishment meets me none the less and as it were reminds me of the execration, the divine curse, the threat of which has been removed from me. Eternal punishment, which is foreshadowed in my temporal experiences, which in fact has already begun relentlessly to overtake me in them, is, so to speak, turned away from me at the last moment by God Himself. And so temporal punishment, without prejudice to its deep seriousness as a foreshadowing of eternal punishment, acquires a new meaning and a new and special complexion: " 'My son, do not regard lightly the discipline of the Lord, nor lose courage when you are punished by Him. For the Lord disciplines him whom He loves, and chastises every son whom He receives'. It is for discipline that you have to endure. God is treating you as sons; for what son is there whom his father does not discipline?" (Heb. 12:5ff.)

Again, such an insight into the meaning of temporal punishment flows from the self-understanding of faith. Only on the basis of such an understanding of our experience in faith are we in a position to assess the value and appropriateness of these sentences; but again, only when we realize that we lie under the shadow of the wrath of God and are exposed to the possibility of eternal punishment. Only against this background do the verses just quoted from Hebrews appear as something quite other than a very human theory which is the fruit of a harmless theodicy without power to impinge on man. We can understand chastisement as chastisement which truly comes from the eternal Father and Judge and serves to secure our ultimate salvation only when we constantly see it to be a manifestation of that eternal punishment which has been averted from us. Against this background of contemplation, however, the saving meaning of temporal punishment becomes in fact an event in our lives in a way which, once again, is intimated by Psalm 90. For let us not forget that this psalm introduces its theme of man's nothingness and transiency under the title: "Lord, God, Thou art our refuge in all generations. . . ."

148

Theses developed in Chapter 7

23. The proclamation of the divine judgment upon sin (Qu. 10) is already implicit in the proclamation of the concept of sin—so long as sin is understood not as a "subjective condition", but as an actual, an objective disturbance in man's relation to God. Sin ever stands under the judgment of God. From the will to live in separation from God, there flows the necessity of living in separation from God. Judgment is an aspect of sin itself.

24. In order that the grace of God should not be preached as "cheap grace", we must with Question 11 repudiate the speculative resort to the mercy of God, regarded as an objectivized attribute of God juxtaposed to His justice. Whenever the person of the living God is proclaimed, both aspects, justice and grace, are contained and fused in the proclamation. Whenever grace is accompanied by judgment in the proclamation, it is prevented from developing into a mere theory of grace, and so of deteriorating into a type of grace that is cheaply valued.

25. The theme of divine anger provoked by sin (Question 10) brings for the first time under consideration the problem of personality in God. The wrathful judgment of God in fact becomes a concrete reality only in the falsity and distortion which mark human life as it is actually lived, and only from that point of view can it be kerygmatically and convincingly disclosed. However, in contrast to an outlook which limits the theme of judgment to the disclosure of the unreality of man's life, and which proposes to exclude the wrath of God as an anthropomorphic myth, we must hold fast to the doctrine of the wrath of God. For only if God is capable of being affected by sin, is the personal character of the relationship in which faith is rooted preserved.

26. The personality of God, thus maintained, is no matter of analogical transference such as is characteristic of speculative thought, but it is an irreducible aspect of the situation in which faith is involved; a situation which the believer himself understands to be personal, that is, to be determined by decision and responsibility.

27. The distinction between "inborn" and "actual" sins, concerning both of which God is equally provoked to anger, reveals to us the principle of total responsibility. Man can set no limit to his responsibility in the sight of God. He is not a whit less responsible for the sin of which he is unaware than for the sin of which he is fully aware. (Consonantly with our repudiation of that interpretation of the fall of man and original sin which stems from ideas of saving history, "inborn" sin can mean nothing

other than "unrecognized sin" (Ps. 90) and transcendental primal guilt.)

28. The distinction between "temporal" and "eternal" punishment (Qu. 10) shows that the judgment of God involves man's ultimate eternal destiny, and that the misery of ultimate exclusion from God can be foreshadowed in temporal experiences. By his faith in divine forgiveness, the Christian becomes aware that eternal punishment is averted for him, but he is none the less overshadowed by its temporal manifestations. In faith, the possibility lies open to him of understanding and accepting these manifestations as God's loving discipline.

# POSTSCRIPT

# POSTSCRIPT

*What is the meaning of "Disclosure of the Human Situation"?*

IN MY introduction I have set this essay in dogmatic theology within the broad framework of the contemporary theological situation and its urgent problems, that is to say, within the framework of our present theological tendency to turn towards man himself and to strive to attain theological "concretion" or actuality, to strive to attain a word of the Church flowing from the deepest, most intimate knowledge of man, hence highly concrete and authoritative. In what follows I have tried, at least to some extent, and under the guidance of the requirements of proclamation, to bring to light the dogmatic clarification and analysis of human realities, of the phenomena which characterize human life. In performing this task, the idea of "disclosure" or "disclosure of the human predicament" constantly emerged—firstly as a heading for the doctrine of sin implied by the very structure and needs of proclamation, then also in numerous particular passages of thought and formulations. The word "disclosure" thus became a characteristic leading idea of this whole dogmatic undertaking.

One immediately anticipates, however, the objection and the suspicious question which will arise: is not the frequently used conception of "disclosure" a component part of natural theology, or does it not indicate a theology emerging from the "point of contact with human nature" such as is not to be justified in view of divine revelation? Is not the theological thinking of this essay based on the supposition that truth may be disclosed from "beneath", from man himself, and so addressed to man?

This possible, and (so far as I am acquainted with the present position of theological discussions) probable, objection, gives me in conclusion the welcome opportunity of taking a retrospective glance at the ground covered, and justifying the underlying intention of the essay and the continuation of work along these lines.

What then is the meaning of "disclosure"? Firstly, a clear distinction must be made between *disclosure* and *demonstration*. Man who is concerned to grapple with and discover truth demands proof, because he has a critical faculty and would like to feel sure in regard to the business he is investigating. He demands that assertions about truth should be capable of being proved before the tribunal of his own criteria of what constitutes truth and knowledge— criteria which he thinks he has at his disposal. It should be possible in this way to justify and authorize them so that they may then be classed among a series of "correct" statements. This method however only succeeds with respect to a certain section of truth-assertions: those in fact which claim for themselves not so much truth as demonstrable accuracy, hence those which, in virtue of the very claim that they make, have already from the outset been subjected to this tribunal.

We are not here concerned to inquire along what lines and by what right man reaches this position of being the arbiter of truth, and how he gains these criteria. We are concerned only to point out that there obviously are some kinds of truth-assertion which by their very nature elude such demonstration, which in fact are by their very nature undemonstrable. Truth of this character does not allow itself to be summoned before man's tribunal. Instead, it summons man to venture outside the circle of his preconceptions to fulfil its demands, for this truth can only be understood in proportion as it is fulfilled, and the knowledge of it comes only through acknowledgement and submission.

It is to this class of truth that the Gospel of Jesus Christ belongs. And indeed it belongs to this class of truth in quite a pre-eminent sense: for in fact from the outset it makes a clear-cut refusal to be summoned before any human tribunal by causing itself to be proclaimed as the supreme scandal: "to the Jews a stumbling-block and to the Greeks foolishness . . ." Yet this undemonstrability does not contradict the thinker's concern for *disclosure*.

The methodological concept of disclosure is inspired by phenomenology and its maxim: "Let us observe things themselves!" To disclose means to bring to light aspects of the phenomenon itself. We can indeed attempt to control a phenomenon by means of a preconceived doctrine which may (by chance) fit the characteristics of the phenomenon in question, or may not. By this approach, we adjust the phenomenon in such a way as to make it fit in with the doctrine. This method may incidentally result in an apparently (but only apparently) clear representation of the thing with which we are dealing. We may however take the opposite course and allow the phenomenon itself to speak, and reflect upon what it tells us of itself. This method however always implies a certain risk and venture, for in this case we no longer have the thing under our control. We do not know in advance what will be the outcome. That the phenomenon will speak and how it will speak, that it will disclose itself and in what sense, becomes an event which escapes human manipulation.

Now it is just this method which is the unavoidable method in all proclamation and theology. Neither proclamation nor theology may burrow themselves in hard and fast doctrines. but they must hear and heed, they must allow the "thing itself", the matter with which they are concerned, to speak. Nor can we preach and teach the Gospel in the void. We must be guided constantly by phenomena, that is, the phenomena of human realities as we all experience them. Faith is not a doctrinaire set of axioms, to which everything, even if unexamined, must somehow—if necessary with violence—be adjusted. It spells the confidence that the phenomena of human reality will in the light of God appear as what they truly are.

Such emergence of truth is the outcome of the working of the Holy Spirit. It is the Holy Spirit, which means God Himself, who shows us what in the last resort truly is. We preach and we theologize in no other way than under the pre-supposition (and under the reservation) that the Holy Spirit is at work in all our thinking. None the less, or rather precisely because of this trust, we must go on thinking and speaking. For the Spirit wills clarity. The Spirit wills to bring forth the fruit of understanding. And just because of this we must take as our starting point the observation of existential phenomena. For faith is just this: the trust and confidence that it is not for us to bring an already known truth to bear on phenomena, but that within phenomena the truth lies implicit. It is the trust that we do not need, as preachers and theologians, believing in the light of God and His word, to do violence to phenomena themselves. It is the trust that Christ is to be found everywhere because He has already and always come to meet man and has assumed humanity into himself.

But of course this cannot be true apart from faith; it is true only on the presupposition of faith. (It is true not by the presupposition of our personal faith—for how could this be big enough? but by the presupposition that God has spoken, speaks and will speak, and that there has existed, exists and will exist on earth a people of God who give heed to His word in faith.) Were we to start work without this basic faith, we should not be standing in the light, and our eyes would be blind to the illumination, our ears deaf to the speech of the phenomena we try to examine.

It is in this sense that I say: the doctrine that man is a sinner is no empty doctrinal assertion, it is something the truth of which is disclosed by the phenomena of existence itself.

That such disclosure succeeds—both here and in relation to other problems—in bringing us to an apprehension of the truth in Christ, is something that lies under the will of God. It succeeds when He allows His light to shine upon us. But we begin to think under the presupposition that we have already seen the light of God in His word, and that it will perhaps please Him to allow us by grace to see it more and more and ever afresh. *Dominus illuminatio mea—et illuminatio mundi.* The Lord is my light—and the light of the world! But it is just under this presupposition that our thinking is carried out. For this reason the methodological principle of "disclosure" belongs necessarily to the quest of *fides quaerens intellectum.*

# INDEX